AMERICA'S AMAZING AIRPORTS

Praise for America's Amazing Airports

"Airports foster economic growth and provide rural and urban communities access to our nation's robust air transportation system. *America's Amazing Airports* showcases these incredible public resources and highlight their importance to our society."

—Aircraft Owners & Pilots Association–AOPA President and CEO, Mark Baker.

"America's network of more than 5,000 airports, including those supporting general aviation operations, represent a vital link in our nation's transportation and economic systems. Equally important, they create jobs, support community businesses and serve a vital humanitarian role in times of crisis. *Americas Amazing Airports* provides an engaging portrait of these extraordinary facilities in our country's aerial landscape."

—National Business Aviation Association–NBAA President and CEO, Ed Bolen

"We all know the nearby large airports served by the airlines. But, Penny Hamilton also points out how this country is served by a huge network of smaller, general aviation airports. They bring important and sometimes life-saving transportation needs by almost 200,000 smaller planes and business aircraft. All this is made possible by over 5,000 public-use US airports, in addition to our highways and roadways. It is important to note, 'a mile of highway gets you one mile - but, a mile of runway gets you anywhere.'"

—Phil Boyer, Aviation Industry Leader

"Our home at one of the most recognized airports in the world–Oshkosh–shows the community and possibilities that local airports create. Any opportunity to share the story of legendary airports, such as in this book, is a pathway to engaging more people in the wonderful world of flight."

—Jack J. Pelton, CEO/Chairman, Experimental Aircraft Association-EAA

"Airports, like airplanes, have personalities. Some are larger than life, others diminutive. But each precious airport is distinct. *America's Amazing Airports* gives us a look at what makes airports–a vital asset of this country–so unique and inspiring."

—Ben Sclair, Publisher, *General Aviation News*.

"*America's Amazing Airports* provides a unique view of airports, guiding the reader through details of today's aviation landscape, and connecting to the pioneers that led to today's safe and efficient airport infrastructure. Airports and access to them are the heart of aviation, allowing flying to be the greatest productivity tool, economic driver, relief mission, and personal time capsule for entrepreneurs and adventurers alike."

—Shelly S. Simi/National Association of State Aviation Officials
NASAO President and CEO

"The airports scattered all across our country are truly amazing places. They whisper, sometimes shout to us incredible stories of personal and corporate growth, success, and sometimes struggle. They reflect American ingenuity, imagination, and sacrifice. By reading *America's Amazing Airports* you can begin to understand the special nature of airports, their impact, and how they have helped shape our nation."

—Kim Stevens, Publisher, State Aviation Journal

AMERICA'S AMAZING AIRPORTS

Dr. Penny Rafferty Hamilton

Mountaintop Legacy Press

America's Amazing Airports

Dr. Penny Rafferty Hamilton

Published by: Mountaintop Legacy Press

Cover Design: Patricia Shapiro Publishing

Print ISBN: 9781699237656

Printed in USA

This book is dedicated to my mentor, best friend, and husband, William A. Hamilton, Ph.D.

Contents

CHAPTER VII

INTRODUCTION

America's airports are relatively young. Prior to 1903, they were unheard of. But, after the Wright Brothers made their historic first powered flight, pilots needed places to take off and land their aeroplanes (what we now call airplanes). At first, pilots used grass strips or dirt fields. But eventually, airfields, airstrips, aeroports, and aerodromes became known simply as airports.

In the early years, open areas such as horse racing tracks and fair grounds were used. Anywhere big enough to gather a crowd to watch the sky for the next act of aerial magic. Sometimes pilots would fly very low down the main streets to announce their arrival and create excitement. Just after World War I, many "Barnstormers" literally descended on more rural areas by "buzzing" over the town and landing near barns in open farm fields.

At first, airplanes were viewed as thrilling entertainment. The lack of reliability of the early aircraft added an element of danger. Soon, traveling pilots formed "Flying Circuses" that began to appear across the United States. To encourage improvements in aircraft safely, a number of cash prizes were offered. As safety improved, the utility of air travel started to become evident.

Just as America's early aircraft were rudimentary, America's road network was not much better. Poor roads, that too often led to even worse roads, sparked the thought, "A mile of road will only take you one mile. But a mile of runway could take you everywhere." That truism led to the creation of America's amazing airports and to the world's greatest air transportation system.

By 1918, scheduled US Post Office Airmail Service was established. Communities quickly realized they needed to build landing sites to accommodate this new and important delivery service or their town would be left in the "horse and buggy age." Airmail played a critical role in demonstrating the commercial use of the increasingly reliable airplane.

As the transcontinental airmail services expanded in the 1920s, towns along the airmail routes quickly built landing sites and refueling facilities. By the early 1930s, the US Government was helping selected towns improve their fledgling airports. In the wake of the Great Depression, more and more towns expanded their airport facilities with the help of the Federal Government New Deal programs. For example, the Works Progress Administration (WPA) improved runways and built airport terminals. Community leaders began to see having a first-class airport as a measure of their vision and leadership. Having a safe airport became a source of community pride.

World War II set off a boom in airport construction across the nation. Especially, in those areas where primary military flight instruction could be conducted in year-round fair weather. Existing airports everywhere were expanded and improved. But, the end of World War II did not mean the end of airport construction and improvements. By the 1960s, the advent of jet-powered aircraft made longer runways a necessity. Soon, new amenities, such as restaurants, shopping areas, and even entertainment facilities began to be part of the airport environment. Today, some of the larger airports have upscale hotels included in the airport terminal itself. To add to a sense of community pride, many airports add the name of a local hero to the name of their airport.

America's amazing airports come in many sizes. For most people, the airports that typically come to mind are the large, Commercial Service airports. Those with airline passenger services, car rentals, control towers, and large bustling terminals. But, in reality, most of our airports in our nation, are smaller General Aviation or Community Airports. Many of these airports do not have or need control towers because they are pilot-controlled. Most of these airports are "public-use airports," meaning all aircraft are welcome. Some, however, are privately-owned and may or may not be open to public use. But, all of America's over 5,000 airports are important to our national aviation transportation system. And, this number does not count the thousands of rural and mountain landing fields.

America has a network of public, private, joint-use, and military-use airports. The United States has approximately one third of the world's airports, the most of any single country.

CHAPTER I

WORLD OF AIRPORTS

The word, "airport" has become so familiar to many Americans that the "port" part is sometimes overlooked. But, with regard to ships that sail the seas, the "port" in seaport, as a place of maritime commerce, is universally understood. Yet, airports are also ports in the truest sense of the word "port." And every community, no matter how far inland can have its own "port." In fact, some airports are so close to the water that they serve as seaports, as well.

COMMERCIAL SERVICE AIRPORTS: In addition to wide, long runways for larger, heavier airplanes for flying passengers all over the world, these airports usually have a terminal building and other facilities in support of passenger and cargo services. International airports have additional customs and passport control services.

EXECUTIVE or BUSINESS AIRPORTS are often located near larger metropolitan areas. For example, Houston Executive Airport (KTME) caters to energy-related business leaders. Because of its business district location, Orlando Executive Airport (KORL) provides quick access to the many corporate headquarters located there. Sometimes, when a metro area's primary Commercial Service Airport needs overflow assistance, these airports are designated as "reliever airports." During adverse weather conditions, reliever airports can be used to improve air-traffic management for the entire system.

GENERAL AVIATION AIRPORTS: Also called GA Airports or Community Airports provide local communities with access to life-saving emergency medical services, medivac flights, and fire fighters. GA Airports link local businesses to our national commerce. They provide a home base to local pilots and are, most often, the first place where future airline pilots and even military aviators learn to fly. GA Airports are the local on-ramp for access to the highways-in-the-sky—our national air transportation network.

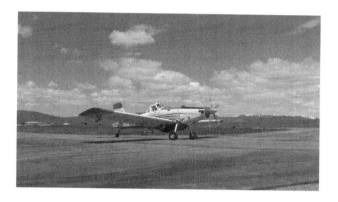

Most General Aviation airports have asphalt or concrete runways.

Some only have gravel or grass landing strips.

HELIPORT is an airport just for helicopters or rotorcraft. Helicopters are very versatile and capable of landing at airports and open, remote areas. Heliport landing pads are marked with a big 'H' inside a circle. Medical facilities often have heliports and many metropolitan areas offer this important landing facility.

JOINT-USE AIRPORTS are shared by both military and civilian aircraft. Joint-use airports are found across the nation, to include Hawaii. Airbases owned and operated by our Armed Forces are usually strictly for the use of military aircraft; however, in emergency situations, non-military aircraft are often allowed to land.

SEAPLANE BASES: These are a type of airport located on a body of water, usually a lake or river, although a few are found in ocean-side harbors. A seaplane or floatplane base offers fuel and other services. Floatplanes sit on large floats. Some floats have wheels that can be extended for use on land, making them amphibious. The floats can be removed for strictly land operations. True seaplanes are a combination of airplane and boat. Most models are not amphibious; however, a few seaplanes have wheels that can be extended down through the aircraft hull.

Tavares, Florida, celebrates their Lake Dora water access with a seaplane base (FA1) and recreational boating marina. America has about sixty-five seaplane bases located across the nation.

GLIDERPORTS: Airports dedicated to gliders or sailplanes are known as Gliderports. Sailplanes typically have long wings to soar on wind currents. Usually, they are not powered by an engine. Gliders are aerodynamically streamlined with thin wings to naturally sail on rising air currents. This glider will be launched into the sky by a powered-aircraft called a tow plane.

RESIDENTIAL AIRPARKS: America has over 400 "Fly-in Communities." These special airparks are found nationwide with homes built around their airport. Hangar-homes are planned to have direct runway or taxiway access to their airport runway. The highest numbers of residential airparks are located in Florida, Washington, California, and Oregon. In addition to aviation, some offer equestrian, golf, and other amenities to airpark homeowners. A newer Ohio residential community, called Sandy's Airpark, is located at the Clermont County/ Sporty's Airport (I69) with the well-known Sporty's Pilot Shop. Fly-in communities celebrate living with airplanes.

CHAPTER II

IN THE BEGINNING

On December 17, 1903, Ohio brothers, Orville and Wilbur Wright, took to the sky at Kitty Hawk, North Carolina, flying a self-propelled, heavier-than-air plane. Little did they know their twelve-second flight over some windswept sand dunes would eventually connect once remote places through a world-wide airport system.

The Wright Brothers Memorial historic site at Kill Devil Hills, North Carolina, can be toured today. The First Flight Airport (KFFA) is public-use and owned by the National Park Service.

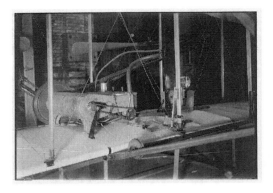

After their historic 1903 flight, the Wrights continued to improve the aerodynamic design of their airplane in their Dayton, Ohio, machine shop.

The Wrights created one of America's first "airports" near their Dayton home called Huffman Prairie Flying Field. After about 150 flights on the Huffman Field, a dependable, fully-controllable airplane emerged called the Wright Flyer III. The Wrights trained others to fly at their Wright Flying School. Many of those graduates joined the Wright Exhibition Team. Early military aviators, Henry "Hap" Arnold and Thomas

Dewitt Milling, were taught by the Wrights. In 1917, the United States Army Signal Corps purchased the Huffman Prairie Flying Field and renamed it, along with adjacent acres, Wilbur Wright Field. In 1948, this historic site was merged with nearby Patterson Air Force Base. Today, a replica hangar and catapult recreates those early days. This site is part of the Dayton National Aviation Heritage Historical Park. In 1990, it was designated a National Historic Landmark. Today, Huffman Prairie Flying Field in located on Wright-Patterson Air Force Base.

As airplane design improved, more intrepid pilots and passengers took to the air. They needed a field or open area to take off and land. Early aviators had keen eyes for potential landing spots. Flat, smooth stretches of land were viewed as potential airfields. Forested areas and corn fields presented hazards to the pilots, passengers, and the flimsy fabric-covered aeroplanes. It became obvious over the years that safe, designated airfields were needed for air transportation to grow and prosper.

Wittemann Bros. Airplane of 1909.

In 1905, early aeronautical engineers and builders, the Wittemann brothers, Charles, Paul, and Walter, opened the first airplane manufacturing plant in the United States on their Staten Island family estate. After experimenting with gliders, in 1906, they designed and built their first airplane. They continued to manufacture a number of experimental planes and models until their ever increasing production forced their move to a larger New Jersey building on the north edge of the Newark meadows. In 1917, they built a new Teterboro Airport plant. There the Wittemanns received the consent of the US Army to convert unused DH-4 aircraft for US Post Office use for the first airmail service. The Wittemann plant modified the planes to carry four hundred pounds of mail. By 1919, further improvements accommodated 1,000-pound payloads. About seventy-five airmail planes were produced at Teterboro Airport. Over the years, several other airplane manufacturing plants located on the airport. During World War II, the US Army operated the airport. Today, Tererboro Airport (KTEB) is the oldest operating in the New York City area. It employs over 1,000 people and provides important aviation services to the entire metropolitan area.

Curtiss machine used by him in his flight from Albany to New York, May 29, 1910. The hydrosurface in the picture were removed and floats substituted for the flight.

As early as 1904, Glenn Hammond Curtiss was involved in engine manufacturing. In 1908, he joined Alexander Graham Bell in pioneering aviation research. By 1916, he formed the Curtiss Aeroplane and Motor Company. A key player in aviation, he provided training for military pilots and aircraft. The Curtiss JN-4, two-seat biplane was the only mass-produced American airplane to play a major World War I role. Affectionately called the "Jenny," many became available after World War I as surplus which helped fuel the post-war barnstorming craze. In 1929, this legacy aviation company merged with the Wrights to create Curtiss-Wright Corporation.

At the September, 1910, Harvard-Boston Aero Meet, the Boston Globe newspaper offered a $10,000 cash prize, which would be over $250,000 in today's dollars. An additional $50,000 in prize money was awarded for duration flights, landing accuracy, and other aviation feats. A 500-acre tract on the Squantum Peninsula near Quincy was the actual site. The promoters announced the thirty-plus-mile flight course from Soldier's Field to the Boston Light, which included a water crossing. By today's standards it sounds easy. Back then, aeroplanes were very flimsy and often unreliable.

On October 14, 1910, English aviation pioneer, Claude Grahame-White, flew his Farman biplane down Washington's Executive Avenue, landing near the White House. Already an accomplished European aviator, he won the Gordon Bennet Aviation Trophy a few days later at the Belmont Park International Aviation Competition. Originally, the building on the left in this photograph was the State, War, and Navy Building. Later, called the Executive Office Building, but now, renamed the Eisenhower Executive Office Building. It is adjacent to the West Wing of the White House.

Nineteen-ten was an important year of "American air awareness" because of large aero-tournaments held in Los Angeles, Boston, and New York. The October 22–30, International Aviation Tournament at the famous New York Belmont horse racing track drew over 150,000 spectators. Over $75,000 in prize money, which is the equivalent of over $2,000,000 today, was awarded. In 1910, the average worker in the United States made twenty-two cents per hour. Only 8 percent of American homes had a telephone. America had a total of 8,000 cars and only 144 miles of paved roads. Automobile fuel was only sold in drug stores. Most cities had a maximum automobile speed limit of only ten miles an hour. Airplanes were a miracle. Americans were fascinated with aeroplanes and pilots at these spectator aviation events.

On August 1, 1911, Journalist, Harriet Quimby, earned Aero Club of America pilot license #37. She became the first US woman to be licensed. She was inspired by the New York Belmont Air Tournament pilots the year before. She joined the Moisant International Aviators Exhibition Team. The media described Quimby as the "Dresden China Aviatrix," because she was petite, pretty, and fair-skinned. She was a huge crowd favorite on the flying circuit. A major sponsor, the Armour Meat Packing Company of Chicago, launched their grape soda, Vin Fiz, with Quimby in her purple satin flying suit gracing the label. On April 16, 1912, Quimby became the first female pilot in the world to fly across the English Channel. She flew a Bleriot monoplane, which would have been front-page news had the Titanic not sunk to the bottom of the ocean the day before her historic feat. Bold and beautiful, she inspired many to fly.

Beachey at Chicago Meet, Aug. 12-20, 1911.

At the 1911 Chicago International Aviation Meet, large crowds continued to flock to see the new flying machines. Pioneer Aviator, Lincoln Beachey, even raced a train. The brave and daring pilot thrilled the huge gathering when he touched his airplane wheels on the top of the moving train as it passed underneath his plane. Flying exhibitions were becoming big business and award money was significant. Many aviation pioneers became famous and wealthy. Often, they died very young because of pushing beyond their own limits and that of their newly designed airplanes.

Leading up to America's World War I entry, very few military or private airfields were developed. Instead, open fields, race tracks, and fair grounds were used. Aviation meets became well-publicized events known months in advance. After the aviation extravaganza, the sites went back to being a park or race track. Shared-use worked for a while. Once America had a need for trained military aviators, the US government began steps to build and partner with communities for flying fields. Before and after World War I, the US War Department Army Air Service wanted a nationwide network of "airdromes," which were more than a place to land and take off safely. The vision was for hangars, refueling, and, even repair facilities. After World War I, many experienced Army Air Corps pilots played a much larger role in airport development. One of their many experienced military aviators was Albert D. Smith. In 1916, he set an American Hydroplane record. The military pushed for airfields as part of our national defense.

Also, in post-World War I America, surplus military flying machines were sold to former military pilots and aspiring adventurers, who took to flight in these bargains. They spread the "Gospel of Aviation" far and wide. They accelerated America into a new and exciting 20th Century. Barnstormers flew around the country giving exhibitions of flying, parachuting, and thrilling airplane rides.

Lincoln Beachey was a pioneer barnstormer. He became an aviation superstar. Famous and wealthy from flying exhibitions, he performed aerial stunts and aerobatics. Estimates are that over 17 million people saw him fly. At the time, the population of the entire United States was just 90 million people. His achievements include inventing figure eights and the vertical drop. He was also the first pilot to achieve terminal velocity by flying straight toward the ground. Several pilots died trying to imitate him. He was known as "The Man Who Owns the Sky," and sometimes, as the "Master Birdman." Beachey is also called the "Father of Aerobatics."

Barnstorming was performed not only by former military men, but also by women and minorities. Bessie Coleman, the first African-American woman to be licensed, thrilled audiences with her air show. She became a role model for many trying to overcome contemporary stereotypes. She used her earned celebrity and wealth to establish a flying school for African-Americans. Initially, barnstormers were most often solo acts. But soon, traveling pilots and aviation entrepreneurs organized Flying Air Circuses to entertain crowds all over America. This aviation show business became the first major form of American civil aviation. Flying circus performances became a popular form of entertainment during the Roaring 1920s.

Bessie Coleman demonstrated how minority women could fly as well as anyone. She was often called "Queen Bessie" because she ruled the sky.

During these early years, aviation and established landing sites were slowly developing across America.

As early as 1909, College Park Airport was established by the US Army Signal Corps as a training location for Wilbur Wright to instruct two military officers to fly the government's first airplane. As early as December 1910, other civilian aircraft began flying at College Park Airport. In 1912, US Army pilot, Lt. Thomas DeWitt Milling, tested a Curtiss military plane at College Park airport.

Although often debated, Maryland's College Park airport claims the prestigious honor of being recognized as our first airport still in continuous operation. College Park Airport (KCGS) has space for more than a hundred aircraft. In 1977, due to its obvious historical and cultural significance, it was listed on the American Register of Historic Places.

In 1905, Pearson Field Airport (KVUO) in Vancouver, Washington, had a dirigible or airship landing. An airship is a gas-filled aircraft that is powered, steerable, and lighter-than-air. By 1911, airplanes began using the airfield. The airport is still in use. In 2012, the American Institute of Aeronautics & Astronautics (AIAA) named it an historic aerospace site.

On May 20–21, 1927, early barnstormer and US Airmail pilot, Charles Lindbergh, changed the world forever when he flew solo, non-stop across the Atlantic Ocean from New York to Paris in his plane, the Spirit of St. Louis. Earlier, New York hotelier, Raymond Orteig, prompted by the Aero Club of America, offered the $25,000 Orteig Prize, which is over $350,000 today, to the first pilot to successfully unite America and Europe by air. Even before he landed in Paris, Lindbergh immediately became an International celebrity. Lindbergh used his fame to promote aviation safety and airport improvements. Building America's airports became a prime focus all across our nation.

CHAPTER III

THE BUILDING YEARS

Powerful tailwinds of change shaped the building of a national airport system. The War Department and the Army Air Service wanted landing fields nation-wide as a matter of national security and defense. The US Postal Department's airmail service provided proof that a national airport system was needed for commerce and industry to thrive.

US Army pilots scouted and created the airmail routes. In 1920, a 2,680-mile transcontinental airmail route linking New York with San Francisco was completed. Initially, mail was flown by day and carried on trains at night. It took three and one-half days for airmail to be sent across our nation, which was still quicker than the all-ground route. The post office was eager to partner with towns with rail connections. In September 1920, when a transcontinental airmail route began deliveries, mail pilots flew in daylight to meet a train at dusk to transfer the mail. Then, the next morning, another mail plane and pilot would meet the train, load up mail sacks to fly on the route. Because of adverse weather and unreliable airplanes, many brave pilots lost their lives as they tried to stay on schedule to make their rail connections.

Some political leaders questioned the practicality of national airmail service. But, the Post Office wanted to prove that mail could be delivered across the county, even at night. In February, 1921, despite winter storms, they began the daring experiment of pilots flying day and night across America from San Francisco to New York. This was a huge test of aviators, aircraft, and community determination. A relay team of airmail pilots flew from city to city.

North Platte, Nebraska, was selected as one of the relay stops. Because North Platte already had a strong railroad line connection, private investors built the airfield with airmail service in mind.

On that cold February night, the entire town of North Plate went to their new airport to help. Nebraskan, James Herbert "Jack" Knight, waited for the airmail plane to arrive from Cheyenne. By hosting this epic night flight, every citizen knew they were playing a significant role in American aviation history. Burning barrels of fuel set the winter sky ablaze as the locals waited for the expected landing. Although the airmail plane was late, after refueling and a few repairs to the airplane, Jack Knight flew off at 10:44 p.m. for Omaha, the next stop.

Knight, a former Army flight instructor, and experienced airmail pilot, lived in Omaha. He had flown to Omaha many times before. But, never at night. Along the route to Omaha, Nebraska towns lighted bonfires to mark his flight path. Despite being exposed to the elements in his open cockpit airplane, a wind-chilled, dehydrated, famished, and exhausted Knight landed in Omaha after 1:00 a.m.

On arrival, Knight was told there was no pilot available to continue the historic night flight to Chicago. Therefore, the success of the airmail experiment depended upon him. Well, Knight said, "The mail must get through." Although he had never flown east of Omaha in the dark, an exhausted Jack Knight took off for the unknown. Fortunately, rural communities stayed awake to light his way. Knight landed in Iowa City to warm up and confirm where he was. Taking off again, Jack reached Chicago Checkerboard Field at 8:40 a.m., just in time to hand the mail off to the next pilot.

When the airmail was delivered to New York, those who doubted began to change their minds about the future of aviation. Landing sites and navigation aids began to appear across the nation. By the mid-1920s, transcontinental airmail routes were supported by a federal navigation beacon program. Often the rotating beacons were augmented by large, concrete arrows pointing the way to the next beacons and set of arrows.

In 1925, the National Air Mail Act, called the Kelly Act, became law. The act provided a legal basis for contracts between the Post Office Department and individual air carriers. This system stimulated America's fledgling airports and airlines. Jack Knight worked with the Postal Service and national civic leaders to extend the system of navigation beacons and landing sites. Later, Knight became a Vice President of United Airlines. To qualify for airmail service, the Post Office specified that airports must have two runways set at right angles to each other. In addition, a tall tower topped by a powerful revolving beacon was required.

By 1924, the most common design of airmail airfield stations was a 2,000-foot by 2,000-foot square of flat terrain. Pilots could land and take off to suit the wind direction. To provide drainage, airport surfaces were spread with gravel or cinders. Typically, the early airports had a hangar, a fuel pump, a wind sock, a telephone connection, and a location marker. For the most part, private and municipal airports copied the square design of the US postal air stations. Some private or city airports even built actual runways lined up with the prevailing wind and with a crosswind runway.

In early 1928, Albany municipal airport was conducting airmail operations. Then, in October, passenger services began. Albany International Airport (KALB) is one of the oldest municipal airport in the United States. Most flying still took place in daylight when pilots relied on the practice of writing numerals, messages, or symbols on rooftops or hillsides to direct them toward the nearest airport. Often, pilots would follow roads or railroad tracks to navigate from town to town. In the 1930s, some local towns painted their name on their water towers.

By the mid-1930s, the Federal Bureau of Air Commerce National Air Marking Program formalized the process. Blanche Noyes, one of America's most celebrated female pilots and aviation leaders, worked tirelessly in this area of aviation safety and air navigation. As head of the federal air-marking division, her job was to train others to paint town and airport names, directional arrows, mileage, and, later, latitudes and longitudes on rooftops. Before World War II, Noyes and her colleagues had over 13,000 air markers painted. After Pearl Harbor, the Civil Aeronautics Administration (CAA) feared air makings could possibly aid enemy pilots, it mandated the obliteration of all air markings that could possibly aid enemy pilots. It took nearly a month to cover up most, but not all, of the airport markings. After the war, airport air markings resumed and continues today. Some airports paint their parking aprons and hangar roofs with their airport identifier.

Before radio navigation aids became available, rotating beacons were installed at ten-mile intervals along major air routes providing night navigation aid. By 1946, the US system consisted of over 2,000 airway light beacons that defined 124 air routes. But, because of weather limitations and because the lighted beacons were only useful at night, radio-based navigation aids were developed. In 1927, the first aircraft radio beacon designed for guiding civilian airplanes by radio was installed at College Park Maryland airport. This served as a forerunner of forty other similar installations strategically placed at 200-mile intervals along America's civil airways.

The 1930s saw the introduction of the Ford Trimotor and, the Douglas DC-2 and DC-3 passenger airliners, the advent of female air stewardesses, and even air travel by First Lady Eleanor Roosevelt. These factors accelerated airline growth which encouraged airport development.

Airmail, even into the late 1930s and 1940s, continued to drive airport and navigation improvements, particularly in the Midwest and western United States. By 1953, the Post Office Department began transporting ordinary letters by air on a space-available basis on airliners. By 1975, air transportation had become so commonplace that all domestic first-class mail was flown as airmail. In 1977, airmail as a special delivery option was officially discontinued.

Prior to World War II, most airports were funded by private owners-investors or by municipalities pressured by their Chamber of Commerce to have faster mail service and more economic growth. Consequently, a nationwide system of airports began to take shape. As airport numbers grew across the United States, safety standards needed to be developed.

In 1926, Congress passed the Air Commerce Act. President Calvin Coolidge established federal control over civil aviation. The act instructed the Secretary of Commerce to foster air commerce, designate and establish airways, establish, operate, and maintain aids to air navigation, arrange for research and development to improve such aids, license pilots, issue airworthiness certificates for aircraft and major aircraft components, and investigate accidents.

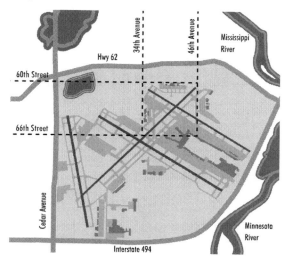

Instead of sharing land with fair ground and race tracts, airports were becoming stand-alone facilities. Ironically, in 1921, a group of investors and several civic organizations joined forces to take control of the bankrupt Speedway Race Track for a new Minneapolis St. Paul Airport (KMSP), calling it, "Speedway Field." Later that year, the new airport was renamed Wold-Chamberlain Field to honor World War I pilots, Ernest Groves Wold and Cyrus Foss Chamberlain. The airport became a joint-use, civil-military international airport. In 1969, it was the filming location for the movie, "Airport," which portrayed authentic scenes of airport managers and staff trying to keep their airport open during a major snowstorm, albeit the "snow" was plastic. The Minneapolis-Saint Paul International Airport continues to thrive on the old Speedway Race Track property today.

Aviation in popular culture in the building years of the 1920s to 1940s impacted airport development. In the early years, movies focused on aviation as entertainment, not commerce.

Just as barnstormers and aerial circus pilots reached people through county fairs and air shows, movies found new aviation audiences. Those same daredevils performed aerial magic with stunts captured on film. The excitement of flight was highly appealing to movie directors. An elite corps of cinematic stunt pilots became world-famous through the movies. Names as Dick Kerwood, Al Wilson, Frank Tomick, Ormer Locklear, and Dick Grace were plastered on movie bills and marques. During those years, non-aviator movie directors required retake after retake of breathtaking air stunt, taking a heavy toll on stunt pilots and aircraft. It is no wonder movie stunt pilots became known as the "Squadron of Death."

As the 1920s came to a close, aerial sequences in films were becoming more common and more spectacular. One outstanding example was *Wings* (1927). Directed by William Wellman, a decorated World War I pilot and the first American to join the Lafayette Escadrille. His film, *Wings*, is considered by historians to be the last great silent epic. In fact, it was the winner of the very first Academy Award for Best Picture. The aerial dog-fighting, bombing raids, and accurate re-creation of combat in *Wings*, were directed by someone who actually lived through it all. The famous Dick Grace was just one of several stunt pilots selected to perform some very dangerous aerial maneuvers.

One of the top stunt fliers of his day, Grace had earned a reputation for skillful aerial work that spanned many years. When Grace saw the deteriorated World War I-era planes that were going to be used in the epic film, he had skilled engineers work with him to rebuild the aging French SPADs and German Fokkers. Once the repairs were complete, Grace expertly weakened in certain places the ones he would use so they would come apart on impact.

In the early 1930s, just as aviation technology improvements were constant, Hollywood moved on from silent films to "talkies" or films with sound. Aviator, Howard Hughes, directed the epic World War I aviation film, "Hell's Angels," which was originally a silent movie. He had it remixed with new footage to become a sound film. Several pilots died during the film, which cost over $4,000,000 to produce. Even though "Hell's Angels" was one of the highest grossing films of the early sound era, Hughes and his investors lost money.

Despite the millions of dollars lost during the Great Depression, improved aviation safety and technological progress were propelling a need for improved airports. In 1928, the first permanent hard-surface runway was built at New Jersey's Newark airport. Although, Henry Ford may have built a hard-surfaced runway earlier in Dearborn, Michigan. Even in the 1930s, airport designers were re-thinking runway surfaces, lengths, and passenger amenities. It was obvious grass landing strips were inadequate, but where would the money come from to pave runways and build terminals?

In 1932 America, about 15 million people were unemployed. Many shuffled along in soup and bread lines. In response, President Franklin D. Roosevelt's administration launched several "New Deal" or federal jobs programs which improved many airports. In 1933, the Civilian Conservation Corps (CCC) was authorized to construct airport landing fields. The Civil Works Administration focused on small public projects, including airport improvements.

The federal Public Works Administration (PWA) built the classic art deco terminal at the Houston Municipal Airport (KHOU), now William P. Hobby airport 1940 Air Terminal Museum. The oldest commercial airport in the Houston area.

The New Deal Works Progress Administration played a major role in airport expansion across the nation. In Colorado alone, WPA built or improved twenty-one community airports to include the Army Air Corps Lowry Airfield in Denver. On December 2, 1939, New York's new municipal airport, LaGuardia, was opened with a paved WPA-built 6,000-foot runway, the nation's longest.

Designed and built as a WPA project, LaGuardia Airport's (KLGA) Marine Air terminal art deco interior is one of New York City's most noteworthy. The mural, "Flight," adorns the wall of this building's circular waiting room. The mural was representative of many of the art works created by the New

Deal Federal Arts Project, a Depression-era program to put artist back to work. Moreover, this building is one of the few surviving examples of air terminals specifically planned in the late 1930s to service "Clipper Ships," which were luxurious seaplanes purpose-built for trans-Atlantic crossings.

Pan American World Airways or Pan Am was a leader in Clipper Ship service and passenger luxury. In the 1930s, Pan Am built their first US land-based International airport in Miami. Pictured is the door of their Pan Am Miami terminal. Pan Am Clipper service was modeled after the world's greatest ocean liners. But, much faster! Pan Am's flying boats provided first-class service to any city with a sheltered harbor, the Clipper Service became extremely popular with well-heeled world travelers.

With the tough economic years of 1929–39, airport terminals along with the views of planes landing and taking off were an inexpensive form of entertainment or escape from the crushing poverty at the time. Art Deco facades and interiors became popular in public building design.

In 1936, Grand Central Air Terminal in Glendale, California, introduced "Streamline Moderne," an international style of Art Deco architecture inspired by aerodynamic design. Streamline architecture emphasized curving forms and long horizontal lines. In industrial design, it was used to give the impression of sleekness and modernity. Another California airline terminal built in this architectural style was Long Beach Airport (KLGB).

In 1936, the Federal Air Traffic Control legislation was passed. On July 6, federal air traffic control began as the Bureau of Air Commerce took over operation of the three airway traffic control stations at Newark, Chicago, and Cleveland. When the Bureau assumed control of the centers, it hired fifteen center employees to become the original federal corps of air-traffic controllers.

Cleveland Municipal Airport, now Cleveland Hopkins International Airport (KCLE), is very important in the history of commercial air travel. Founded in 1925, it was the first municipality-owned facility. In the 1930s, it was the first airport to have a ground-to-air radio-equipped control tower. It was the first airfield to install a runway lighting system.

While New Deal programs saved many airports, the World War II military use of civilian airports helped make them an essential part of our national landscape, forever. For example, in 1936, Bellingham airport, a grass strip runway, was constructed using Works Progress Administration funding. On December 7, 1941, a paved and expanded runway opened on the very same day of the Japanese Pearl Harbor attack. Three days later, the army took over the airport creating Bellingham Army Airfield. Throughout the war years, runways were paved, strengthened, and thirty-eight additional airport buildings constructed to house bombers and fighter planes. By 1946, this greatly improved airport was returned to civil use. Today, that is Bellingham International Airport (KBLI).

This and similar scenarios were repeated across America. In the name of national security, municipal airports were taken over and revitalized with expanded and new infrastructure. Airports, which had been neglected during the Great Depression, were often given new and improved facilities. For example, Wendover Airfield, Utah, played such an historic role in WWII. In the 1940s, the federal government began building bombing ranges nearby. Wendover was perfect because of its topography, weather, and being sparsely populated with only a hundred people. Construction began. When America entered the war, construction boomed.

By 1943, Wendover had over 2,000 civilian employees, 17,500 military personnel, three 8,100 foot paved runways with multiple taxiways, and seven hangars. By 1945, 668 buildings, including a 300-bed hospital, library, chapel, bowling alley, two movie theaters, and 361 housing units. The facilities supported the B-17 Flying Fortress, B-24 Liberator training, and even the "Enola Gay" B-29, the aircraft that carried the nuclear bomb to Hiroshima. Declared surplus in the late 1970s, it is one of our most intact WWII training airfields. By the late 1990s, Toole County Wendover Airport (KENV) preserved its significant role in national aviation history through the Wendover Airfield Museum.

The federal government took an unusual role in building Washington National Airport, now called Ronald Reagan Washington National Airport (KDCA).

As early as 1938, President Franklin D. Roosevelt selected the site for the new Washington National Airport. Although the need for a better airport was acknowledged in thirty-seven different reports conducted between 1926 and 1938, a statutory prohibition against federal development of airports was in place. It literally took an Act of Congress to lift that prohibition. President Roosevelt moved quickly. Through "recess appropriation" of funds allocated to other programs for other purposes, he appropriated $15,000,000 to build National. That would be almost $275,000,000 today. Some in Congress challenged the legality of Roosevelt's actions in court. Nevertheless, construction steamrolled on. President Roosevelt directed the Public Works Administration, Works Progress Administration, Army Corps of Engineers, National Park Service Department of the Interior, and private contractors to spare no effort. Almost 20 million cubic yards of sand and gravel were moved to the new airport. Erosion control and dike construction were completed. Four powerful hydraulic dredges were used to remove silt from the runway beds so the ground could be compacted and stabilized. On September 28, 1940, President Roosevelt laid the terminal building cornerstone.

On June 16, 1941, the new airport called Washington National Airport opened. Based on an earlier agreement, the first airline to land was American Airlines. The pilot of that plane, Bennett H. Griffin, later became the first Washington National Airport manager. On opening day, just one hangar was completed and in operation. Five hangars were under construction with a seventh in the planning stage. Washington National Airport was considered the 'last word' in airports with ultramodern developments in design of buildings, air traffic and ground traffic control, field lighting, and facilities for public passenger comfort and convenience.

By 1958, the first Pan Am Boeing 707 jet was christened at Washington National. By 1966, jet service was operating. In 1967, the grooving of runway 18–36 to improve traction when wet was a first for a civil airport in the United States. In 1998, by another Act of Congress, the airport name was changed to Ronald Reagan National Airport to honor America's 40th President (1981-89).

What might have seemed impossible after that first Wright Brothers flight at Kitty Hawk, was now a reality. By 1953, airports were interconnected to form a web of transportation and commerce for a booming post-World War II economy. By 1958, President Eisenhower signed the new Federal Aviation Act into law, creating an independent Federal Aviation Agency.

Commercial jets, such as the Boeing 707, required longer takeoff distances, causing many runways to be extended in length. In 1962, Washington Dulles International Airport (KIAD) was the first airport built with jet service a design consideration. Technology was rapidly changing airports and the aviation industry.

In the early 1970s, several airlines served unique airports which often had short, single runways called STOLports or Short Take Off Landing. Smaller, propeller aircraft were used to provide commercial airline service to New York City, Los Angeles, and Walt Disney World Resort. Rocky Mountain Airways provided Colorado with commercial airline STOLport service using the Canadian-built, de Havilland DHC 6 and Dash 7. These aircraft were flown to provide airline mountain service to Avon STOLport near Vail, to Granby (KGNB), and Steamboat Springs Airport (KSBS).

America's amazing airports are modern engineering and economic miracles. They transport millions of people. Promote business and economic growth, save lives, protect wildlife and our food supply, provide laws enforcement and fire protection services. However, some of America's airports are in danger of closure by encroaching development and political pressure. Santa Monica Municipal Airport (KSMO), once home to the Douglas Aircraft Company's famous DC-3, is a valuable economic asset and important reliever airport for the busy Los Angeles International Airport (KLAX). However, Santa Monica is scheduled for closure in the near future for development.

Opened in 1995, Denver International Airport (KDEN) is the last major US airport built and also the most expensive. It is North America's largest airport in total land and has the longest public use runway—the 16,000 foot 16R/34L. The terminal roof represents the snow-capped Rocky Mountains and the historic Native American tepees. The space-age Teflon-coated fiberglass roof and catenary steel cable system, similar to that of the Brooklyn Bridge, make an iconic image of modern airport design.

America's airports are funded by the users of our national aviation system through federal and state taxes on aviation fuels, aircraft batteries, and other aviation-related items. In 1971, the Airport and Airway Trust Fund was established. For the most part, the Airport and Airway Trust Fund is funded by a tax on airline tickets. Air freight shipments are taxed, as well. That money is used to improve America's air transportation system by funding airport improvements, airport repair projects, and modernizing our Air Traffic Control system.

Since 1980, airports have received significant capital development funding from the Federal government in the form of Airport Improvement Program (AIP) grants through the Federal Aviation Administration. AIP funds airport construction projects, terminal development, safety and snow removal equipment, weather reporting systems, and many other important airport projects.

Usually a federal AIP grant provides 90 percent of the total project cost. Most often, a state aviation trust fund provides another 5 percent of the funding with the remaining 5 percent coming from local governments or airport authorities. State aviation trust funds receive their funding from fuel taxes paid by private pilots and the airlines. Thus, the world's best airport and airways system is almost entirely funded by those who use our airports and airways. Aviation fuel taxes are collected at the refinery level, a system requiring very few federal or state workers to collect. Also, airports can use a combination of airport cash reserves, debt capital raised in the municipal bond market, commercial loans, and grants from Federal and State governments. The sale of tax-exempt bonds and the provision of Federal AIP grants finance many of America's major airport capital-improvement projects.

CHAPTER IV

AIRPORTS OUTSIDE AND INSIDE

Each industry has special terminology. Airports have a special vocabulary, jargon and technical terms to describe important services and functions. Here are a few examples.

Outside

Aprons are also called airport ramps. An apron is the area on the airport where aircraft are parked, loaded/unloaded, and refueled. Typically the ramp area is more accessible to users than a runway or taxiway. But, with new security regulations, the ramp/apron area is usually not open to the general public. Often, at military airfields and large training airports this area is called the Flight Line.

Beacons signal airport information to pilots flying at night. Older beacons have rotating lights. Newer beacons have flashing lights. Alternating white and green lights communicate the airport is a civilian landing site. Military airport beacons flash two white lights for a single green light. Seaplane beacons flash white and yellow lights. Heliport beacons alternate between green, yellow, and white lights.

Airport Lighting System (ALS) provides glide-slope information to pilots. For example, Visual Glideslope Indicators (VASI)

are light bars on the side of the runway approach. The VASI shown in the photograph is a Precision Approach Path Indicator (PAPI). These devices are housed in a box typically to the left side of the approach end of the runway.

Runway edge lights are steady white lights. Some airports have Sequenced Flashing Lights as part of their instrument-approach lighting system. Flashing strobe lights direct the pilot's eyes to the runway threshold. Pilot slang calls them: "jack rabbit" or "running rabbit" lights.

Blue taxiway edge lights outline the taxiways and are there to assist pilots at night or in conditions of restricted visibility.

Control Towers are major features at Commercial Service and heavy air-traffic airports. They are used to direct the movements of aircraft and airport maintenance vehicles by radio and, sometimes, by light signals. Only around 520 airports have tower-controlled operations. Most airports do not have or need control towers. Pilots use a Common Traffic Advisory Frequency (CTAF) to announce their location with reference to the airport and their intensions for landing and taking off at that airport.

Fuel Farms consist of above or below ground fuel tanks used to provide fuel to aircraft with fuel pumps or via refueling vehicles. Many are self-service, credit card operations.

Hangars provide weather protection and an area for aircraft maintenance and repair. In 1902, the Wright Brothers stored and repaired their glider and Wright Flyer in a wooden hangar constructed at Kill Devil Hills.

Jet Bridge, Jet Way, Aerobridge, and Gangway are terms for covered walkways at a terminal gate, providing passenger access to the airplane cabin for entry and exit. In 1959, the first jet bridge was installed at San Francisco Airport (KSFO).

Runways are specifically defined rectangular surfaces for airplanes to land and take off. Runways are named with a number between 01 and 36 which reflects the runway's magnetic heading in degrees. A runway can generally be used in both directions with each runway end designated by the appropriate number. But, some terrain-restricted runways are one way in and one way out. A runway 09 means the airplane would be headed east. The opposite end would be called 27, meaning the airplane would be headed west.

Runway Threshold is the beginning of the runway landing area for the airport, in pilot slang called "piano keys." The number of "keys" indicates to pilots the runway width.

Taxiways connects airplanes to runways. Taxiway signs direct pilots to and from runways.

Terminals provide passenger facilities, airport administrative offices, and access to ground transportation. Some larger airports have more than one terminal building.

Tie Down Areas are marked on parking ramps. Tie-down rings embedded in the ramp surface protect aircraft from being displaced by high winds and from the propeller wash of taxiing aircraft.

Transient/Maintenance Hangars are important airport structures that provide weather protection for aircraft and provide climate-controlled conditions for aircraft maintenance. Aerogarage was an early name for hangars. Airfields used for US Airmail service were required to have at least one maintenance hangar.

Windsocks are light, flexible fabric cones mounted on a mast to indicate wind direction and velocity. Windsocks offer pilots a quick and easy indication of wind speed and direction on runways. It is important aerodynamically that planes land into the wind. Also, if the wind sock indicates a crosswind, pilots can adjust their landing technique or even fly to another airport with more favorable wind conditions.

Inside

Airport Terminals most often include airline passenger ticketing counters, car rentals, food and beverage services, and airport administrative offices. Where required Transportation Security Administration (TSA) facilities are included.

Airport Security Check Points are the locations where ticketed airline passengers are screened by the TSA. Prior to the 2002

passage of the Aviation and Transportation Security Act, airports had minimal screening procedures. Even as early as the 1970s, airline hijacking indicated the need for more thorough airport security measures.

Baggage Claim areas are where deplaning passengers reclaim their baggage. Some larger airports have baggage carousels. Originally, US Airmail bags were the driving factor for airline development. Transporting passengers was not as important to the nascent airlines. Some early airline passengers found the only place to sit in the airliner was on top of a filled US Mail bag.

Gates are the location that provide airline passengers a place to await their departing flight. Usually, gate agents have ticketing/seating computers, and a public-address system. Often, a jet bridge is connected to the gate. In some locations, passengers walk out the gate to a set of aircraft stairs.

CHAPTER V

SPECIAL AIRPORT AND AVIATION WORDS

Because clear communication is so important to aviation safety, the world of airports and aviation is replete with special words and terminology. Think of these as "airport speak," terms used by airport and aviation professionals to be exact and clear. Many special words are acronyms, a series of letters pronounced as a word. An example is NAVAID which can be pronounced just the way it looks. Some other airport terms are initials that cannot be pronounced as words. The individual letters are sounded out. For example, ADF and NDB. ADF stands for Automatic Direction Finder. NDB means Non-Directional Beacon. While these aviation acronyms are useful among aviators and airport personnel, they are often a secret language to those outside the world of aviation. Here are a few more examples:

Airport Facility Directory (AFD) is a FAA publication detailing the facilities available at each US airport.

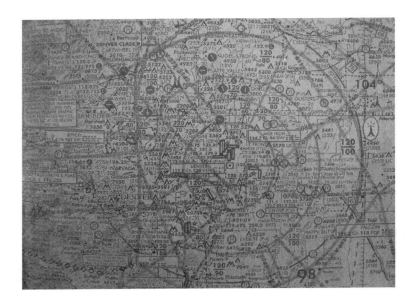

Aeronautical Charts are maps specially designed for aerial navigation. An aeronautical chart is much like a road map used by drivers to navigate.

Airport Identification Code (AIC)–In the 1930s, the US implemented a uniform system that provided each airport with a unique AIC. Often, the first three letters of a town's name were used. For example, ATL is Hartsfield-Jackson Atlanta International Airport. Some airports serve more than one city. An example is DFW, meaning Dallas/Fort Worth International Airport. Some AICs are based on the original name of the airport. For example: the AIC for Chicago O'Hare International Airport is ORD. Why? Because today's O'Hare was built in what used to be an orchard. After World War II, the Orchard Airport was expanded and renamed for the highly decorated hometown hero, Butch O'Hare. But, the original ORD AIC remains the same.

The International Civil Aviation Organization (ICAO) decided each nation should have a unique identifying letter. For all US airports in the lower forty-eight states, the nationality identifier is 'K,' followed by the usual three letter AIC. For international flight-planning purposes, Denver International Airport is KDEN. However, the ICAO AICs for airports in Alaska and Hawaii begin with a 'P,' usually followed by their three letter/digit AIC. Again, every airport in the world is uniquely identified by its own Airport Identifier Code.

Aircraft Rescue and Fire Fighting (ARFF) denotes a special category of fire fighting equipment and personnel training for fighting airport and aircraft fires with special emphasis on passenger and crew rescue from burning aircraft. ARFF standards are mandated at all US airports providing scheduled airline service. ARFF firefighters have advanced training in foam and dry chemical applications to snuff out aviation fuel fires.

Air Traffic Control (ATC)–The Federal Aviation Administration provides ATC services to keep aircraft separated from each other and to regulate the flow of aircraft traffic in and out of congested airspace.

A is ALPHA	B is BRAVO	C is CHARLIE
D is DELTA	E is ECHO	F is FOXTROT
G is GOLF	H is HOTEL	I is INDIA
J is JULIET	L is LIMA	K is KILO
M is MIKE	N is NOVEMBER	O is OSCAR
P is PAPA	Q is QUEBEC	R is ROMEO
S is SIERRA	T is TANGO	U is UNIFORM
V is VICTOR	W is WHISKEY	X is X-RAY
Y is Yankee	Z is ZULU	

Aviation Alphabet—In the 1930s, a standardized phonetic alphabet was developed to insure effective communication. Over the years, it has become known as the NATO (North Atlantic Treaty Organization) Phonetic Alphabet. When clarity is essential, the spelling out of the words over the radio or telephone using the NATO Alphabet has become almost universal.

Aviation Fuel is especially formulated for aircraft use. There are two types: Avgas (100LL) for reciprocating engines and Jet-A (JP-4) which is used in jet engines. The two cannot be mixed. Special fuel nozzles, along with warning placards, are used to prevent fueling mistakes.

Automated Weather Observation Systems (AWOS) are located on or near airports to report real-time weather information. Examples of information reported are: wind direction and speed, horizontal and vertical visibility, outside temperature, and the barometric pressure which is essential to accurate altimeter readings. Each AWOS has a unique radio frequency and a telephone number. The weather data is also available to the general public.

Common Traffic Advisory Frequency (CTAF) is the name given to the VHF radio frequency used by pilots for air-to-air communication at US airports that do not have control towers.

Fixed Base Operator (FBO) is an airport aviation business providing aeronautical services such as fueling, hangaring, aircraft rental and maintenance, flight instruction, and aviation supplies.

Foreign Object Debris (FOD) is an object in an inappropriate airport location that has the capacity to damage an aircraft, airport machinery, or hurt personnel. Examples of FOD are rocks, pavement rubble, nuts, bolts, and litter, in general.

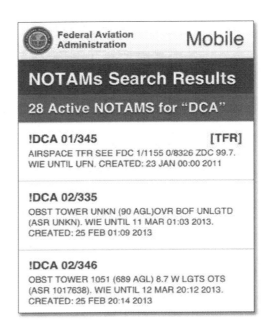

Notice To Airman (NOTAMs) are Federal Aviation Administration special alerts (usually temporary) to pilots about unusual airport conditions such as inoperable navigation aids or lighting, on-airport maintenance operations, such as runway/taxiway striping. BIRDTAMs alert pilots to possible bird strikes. SNOWTAMs alert pilots to possible snow on runways.

Pilot Controlled Lighting (PCL) allows pilots to use aircraft radios to activate runway lighting. The pilot keys the CTAF frequency a certain number of times to turn on the runway lighting and can even adjust the intensity of airport lighting up or down by this method.

Runway End Identifier Lighting (REIL) is a distinctive set of lights to assist pilots with identification of the approach ends of runways.

Tarmac is an older term describing materials patented in 1901 called tarmacadam, a combination of crushed rock and cement, mixed with tar used in the past to surface runways and taxiways.

Universal Communications (UNICOM) is an air-ground-based radio station used by pilots and airport-based businesses, such as a FBO, to arrange for use of the airport courtesy car (if provided) or for car rental, refueling, and other airport services. If a non-towered airport does not have a CTAF, UNICOMs can provide air-traffic updates. But, not air-traffic control.

Very High Frequency (VHF) Omnidirectional Range (VOR) is a type of short-range radio navigation guidance system for aircraft.

Wheel Chocks are wedges of wood, metal, or rubber placed in front and behind an airplane wheel for safety to keep the aircraft from rolling or moving.

Zulu Time–Because modern aircraft can quickly cross from one US time zone into another, confusion is avoided in English speaking nations by the use of Greenwich Mean Time (GMT), which pilots and air-traffic controllers refer to as Zulu Time. Coordinated Universal Time (UTC) is the same as GMT but is the term used where English is not the common language.

CHAPTER VI

MEET AIRPORT PEOPLE

Airports, in particular, and aviation in general, offer unlimited opportunity for careers. Some aviation careers do not require a college degree or advanced education. Moreover, many aviation-related employers offer scholarships and training opportunities. The "magic of flight" makes airports exciting places to work. Here are just a few examples of the careers that make America's air transportation system the world's best.

Air Traffic Controllers help guide airplanes both up in the sky and down to the ground.

Ground Controllers are like traffic cops, using their radios and even signal lights to ensure that airplanes move along the taxiways surely and safely. To be an air-traffic controller, one must be certified by the FAA. Certification is earned by passing a series of examinations and meeting experience requirements. To learn more about ATC opportunities and other positions within the Federal Aviation Administration, visit: www.faa.gov.

Airport Operations Personnel perform a variety of on-airport jobs, such as terminal-building and airport maintenance, landscaping, snow removal, deicing crew, airplane refueling, catering, and sanitation services. Many are entry level positions that provide on-the-job training and the opportunity for upward advancement.

Aircraft Mechanics must have specialized training and meet rigorous FAA standards. For example, the A&P Certificate

(Airframe and Power Plant) or advanced levels. The advent of the Glass Cockpit means Avionics Technicians must constantly upgrade their knowledge and skills. Many scholarships are available to support this field.

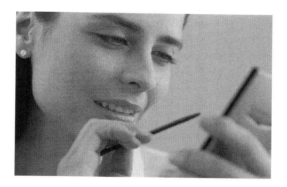

Airport Consultants, Engineers, Marketing and Communication Specialists, and Aviation Writers are just a few other opportunities in the exciting field of aviation and airport management.

In addition to **Airport Managers,** larger airports have marketing, customer service, accounting, human resources, and information technology specialists.

Baggage Handlers load and unload luggage and freight cargo from aircraft. Often, this airport opportunity requires the candidate to be over eighteen years of age, and pass a security and medical checks. On-the-job training is the norm.

Fixed Base Operators (FBOs) often have dispatchers, flight school schedulers, aircraft rental schedulers, accountants, and customer service team members. And, of course, the all-important Certified Flight Instructors (CFIs).

Flight Crews include pilots, copilots, and flight attendants. Airline Cabin Crew members, flight attendants, are primarily responsible for passenger safety.

Food and Beverage businesses play an important role at larger airports. Airline provisioning agents stock airliners and charter aircraft with food and beverages.

Airline Representatives are the gate agents and customer-service representatives. These are jobs that can lead to upper management positions in the airline industry.

Medivac pilots, flight nurses, medical technicians, helicopter mechanics, flight, crew schedulers, and dispatchers staff some of aviation's most rewarding fields.

CHAPTER VII

AIRPORTS HONOR NOTABLE LEADERS

Many airports are named to honor important aviation leaders and local heroes. Savor this national sample:

Alabama: Moton Field-Municipal Airport Tuskegee Airmen National Historic Site (06A) commemorates the important contributions of World War II African-American airmen. In 1915, after the death of founder, Booker T. Washington, Robert Russa Moton, a distinguished African-American educator and author, was named Tuskegee Institute principal. Moton was a visionary leader committed to aeronautical training and engineering. Moton died in 1940, before the Tuskegee Airmen took flight. In 1941, the new training base began teaching African-American men known as the Tuskegee Airmen. They were the first African-American aviation unit in the US Armed Forces. They served in the 332nd Fighter Group and the 477th Bombardment Group of the US Army Air Corps. Tuskegee Airman, Edward C. Gleed, class of 42-K, began as a Tuskegee aviation cadet and graduated in December 1942. He joined the 332nd Fighter Group in Ramitelli, Italy. They earned the unofficial name, "Red Tails," because of the red tails they painted on their P-51 Mustangs. This added to their *espirit de corps* and provided easy recognition. Their primary mission was to escort bombers striking targets in Southern Europe. Tuskegee Airmen earned a stellar reputation for their bravery and aerial skills.

Alaska: Ted Stevens Anchorage International Airport (PANC). Stevens, a World War II Aviator, earned the Distinguished Flying Cross. This important military award is given to a member of our armed forces for heroism or extraordinary achievement while participating in an aerial combat situation. Stevens served Alaska in the US Senate from 1968 to 2009. He had a life-long commitment to aviation. Senator Stevens was named Alaskan of the Century. Built in 1951, the airport is one of the world's largest and busiest floatplane bases. Airports and aviation play a key role in Alaska's economy.

Arizona: Prescott Regional Airport Ernest A. Love Field (KPRC) honors First Lieutenant, Ernest A. Love, decorated World War I pilot shot down near Verdun, France. Local Prescott High School football star, Ernest Love, was named All-State Guard in his junior year. He studied mechanical engineering at Stanford University. After flight training, he was assigned to the 141st Training Squadron. Upon arrival in France, he received advanced flight training. In the summer of 1918, he flew Nieuport 28 fighters. In September, he scrambled in support of American troops on the battle-field in his SPAD fighter, a highly capable, powerful, and popular French airplane. The name SPAD is an acronym derived from the initials of the Societe pour Aaviation et ses Derives. Love was shot down in aerial combat and badly wounded. On September 16, 1918, he died of his wounds in a German field station. His local community honored his service and sacrifice by including Ernest A. Love Field in their airport name. Award-winning Prescott Regional Airport is a vital Arizona transportation hub with a mix of aircraft operations including: flight training, corporate, private, cargo, US Forest Service air tankers, first responder, military, and commercial air service operations.

Arkansas: Bentonville Municipal Airport Louise M. Thaden Field (KVBT). In 1951, the airport was named to recognize the aviation accomplishments of Bentonville native, Louise McPhetridge Thaden. In 1928, Louise earned pilot license number 850, signed by Orville Wright. In 1929, Thaden co-founded the International Ninety-Nines, female pilot organization, with Amelia Earhart and Ruth Nichols. Thaden was the first to simultaneously hold the women's altitude, endurance, and speed records. In 1936, Thaden and her co-pilot, Blanche Noyes, who was Ohio's first licensed female pilot, were the first women to win the coveted Bendix Trophy. Besting the male pilots in that transcontinental New York to Los Angeles National Air Race, flying a Beechcraft model C-17R, "Staggerwing." They completed the air race in just fourteen hours and fifty-five minutes. This annual US aeronautic point-to-point race began in 1931 to foster the design of more reliable aircraft. In 1999, Louise Thaden was inducted into the National Aviation Hall of Fame.

California: Charles M. Schulz–Sonoma County Airport (KSTS) is named in honor of "Peanuts" cartoonist and civic leader, Charles Schulz. His legacy includes the beloved Snoopy, the loyal beagle of Charlie Brown. Snoopy imagines he is a famous British World War I Royal Flying Corps 'Ace.' Snoopy wears his aviator helmet, goggles, and scarf, while flying his Sopwith Camel fighter plane, cleverly disguised as a dog house. He imagines the dreaded German Ace, the "Red Baron," is out there waiting for an aerial dog fight. Schulz developed a cast of whimsical characters known worldwide. Sonoma County Airport serves as an important aviation link to other larger airports.

San Diego International Airport Lindbergh Field (KSAN) honors famed aviator, Charles Lindbergh. He chose San Diego's Ryan Airline Company to custom-build his single-engine, high-wing monoplane called the "Spirit of St. Louis." Lindbergh worked closely with the team, watching Ryan NYP (New York Paris), the official name of the plane, come to life in their skilled hands. After Lindbergh's historic 1927 transatlantic solo flight, San Diego leaders asked him to lend his name to their new and improved airport dedicated on August 16, 1928. San Diego's Lindbergh Field immediately attracted business attention. By 1930, the San Diego to Los Angeles airmail route was initiated. During World War II, the federal government transformed the airport into a modern aviation center. The military built a long runway for heavy bombers. Today, San Diego is our nation's busiest single-runway commercial airport.

Colorado: Granby/Grand County Airport Emily Warner Field (KGNB) is named for Colorado native, Emily Warner. She began her historic aviation career as an accomplished flight instructor. In 1973, Warner was hired by Frontier Airlines as a commercial airline pilot. By 1976, she became America's first female airline Captain, breaking the "glass ceiling of the flight deck" for other American women to become airline pilots. Warner's airline captain uniform is in the Smithsonian Air and Space Museum. Emily always considered Granby/ Grand County Airport as her home. In July, 2015, she was honored when her home airport was named for her and by the establishment of the Emily Warner Field Aviation Museum inside the former Rocky Mountain Airways airline terminal building. The airport has twice been recognized as Colorado Pilots Association General Aviation Airport of the Year. In 2018, the Emily Warner Field Aviation Museum earned a top History Colorado award for its aviation heritage educational programs.

Connecticut: Bradley International Airport (KBDL) has its roots as a 1940s military aviation airport. It bears the name of twenty-four-year-old, Army pilot, Lt. Eugene M. Bradley, who was killed in his Curtiss P-40 Warhawk during a training drill on the field. Today, this is a joint-use civil/military airport. As the second largest airport in the New England area, Bradley International Airport is Connecticut's busiest commercial airport. Along with civilian aircraft, the Connecticut Air Guard and USAF 103rd Airlift Wing use the facility.

Delaware: The first state to ratify our Constitution does not have an airport that provides airline service; however, Delaware has a number of public-use and private General Aviation airports that provide charter flights and many other important agricultural and medical services.

Dover Air Force Base (KDOV) has a large military aviation mission. After the December 7, 1941, Japanese attack on US Naval ships and personnel at Pearl Harbor, the Dover Airdrome-Municipal Airport began to play its role in aviation history when it was converted to military use. In 1948, it was renamed Dover Air Force Base. Over the years, this strategic air base has been improved. In 2009, the original 1955 base air traffic control tower was replaced with a new 128-foot control tower operation center. Dover AFB is a vital part of our air defense. A C-17 Globemaster III is shown about to transport troops from Dover AFB.

Florida: Albert Whitted Airport (KSPG). St. Petersburg is recognized as the birthplace of scheduled commercial airline flight. On January 1, 1914, about 3,000 people watched from the central yacht basin dock as the Benoist XIV St. Petersburg-Tampa Airboat Line, piloted by Tony Jannus, gently lifted off with paying passenger, A.C. Pheil, the former St. Petersburg mayor. The flight to Tampa demonstrated the commercial possibilities of airplanes. In the late 1920s, airport construction began. The airport opened with the name Cook-Springstead tracks. Later, it was renamed to honor Navy Lieutenant, James Albert Whitted, a St. Petersburg native. He was one of the first 250 Naval Aviators commissioned. In 1917, when America entered World War I, Whitted served as chief instructor of advanced flying. In 1919, when he returned home, he introduced flying to the people of St. Petersburg, usually without charge. In 1923, he died in a commercial aviation accident. In 1929, one of the famous airships, the Goodyear Tire and Rubber Company Blimp, was based at Albert Whitted Airport. The airport played an important World War II role as the US Coast Guard Air Station. Rescue, and other life-saving missions continued into the 1970s. Today, Albert Whitted Airport serves its community with strong General Aviation, air-taxi, helicopter, and business aviation services.

Georgia: Athens-Ben Epps Airport (KAHN) is named for Ben T. Epps. As early as 1907, Epps designed and built a series of monoplanes. Epps is considered Georgia's first aviator. In 1917, he opened the airport. Today, this airport continues to serve a vibrant and growing General Aviation community.

Hawaii: Daniel K. Inouye International Airport (PHNL) is one of our largest, busiest, and most beautiful airports. In 2017, it was named to honor Medal of Honor recipient and Hawaii's former US Senator (1963–2012), Daniel K. Inouye. In 1927, this historic airport opened as John Rodgers Airport, honoring a World War I naval officer. Funded by the Chamber of Commerce and territorial legislature, it became Hawaii's first full airport. After December 7, 1941 with the Japanese attack at Pearl Harbor, the US military grounded all civil aviation and took over Rodgers airport, converting it to Naval Air Station Honolulu. Significant infrastructure was built during the war years to include a terminal building, control tower, upgraded runways and an improved seaplane base. In 1947, the airport returned to civil use and was renamed Honolulu Airport, with the word, "International," added in 1951. In 1959, jet service began. Later, with modernization and expansion, a new John Rodgers Terminal continued to honor the airport's history. Constructed in 1997, the Reef Runway holds a unique place in aviation history as the world's first runway constructed entirely off shore.

Idaho: Coeur d'Alene Airport/Pappy Boyington Field (KCOE) was built in 1942 by the Army Corps of Engineers. In 2007, it was named to honor native son and highly decorated World War II Marine Corps combat pilot, Gregory "Pappy" Boyington, recipient of the Medal of Honor. Boyington commanded the World War II Marine Fighter Squadron VMF-214. Because they were not originally assigned to a unit or ship, had few reliable planes, and no mechanics, they adopted the name, "Black Sheep Squadron," conveying they were illegitimate or orphans. They were outstanding aviators. Their record number of nine aces with numerous confirmed air-to-air victories put them in elite status. In 1958, Boyington wrote his memoir, Baa Baa Black Sheep. Later, a popular television program, based loosely on his autobiography, aired in 1976 to 1978. The opening credits read: "In World War II, Marine Corps Major Greg 'Pappy' Boyington commanded a squadron of fighter pilots. They were a collection of misfits and screwballs, who became the terrors of the South Pacific. They were known as the Black Sheep." Today, Boyington is honored at the Coeur d'Alene Airport in bronze.

Illinois: O'Hare International Airport (KORD) is named for Chicago's World War II US Navy Ace, Edward "Butch" O'Hare, a Medal of Honor recipient. The origin of aviation "Ace" began in 1915. During the World War I stalemate, a French newspaper described French aviator and flight instructor, Adolphe Pegoud , as"l'As" or "the Ace." Needing a hero, the French immediately embraced the cult of "the Ace," defined as a military pilot with at least five enemy planes shot down. O'Hare Airport was the first major post-World War II airport to be named for an Ace. In 1955, commercial service officially began. O'Hare with its concourses, direct highway terminal access, jet bridges, plus shopping and food amenities set the standard for future airports. During 1963 to 1998, Chicago O'Hare International was described as the World's Busiest Airport.

Indiana: Indianapolis International Airport (KIND), formerly Weir Cook Municipal Airport, opened in 1931 with a price tag of $724,000. Or, about $12,000,000 in today's dollars. The original terminal building alone cost $125,000, which would be about $2,000,000 today. Named to honor aviation legend, Harvey Weir Cook, an Ace who flew in the famed World War I 94th Aero Squadron. This all-volunteer aviation unit was the first American squadron to fly and fight on the Western Front in Europe. The squadron adopted the "Hat in the Ring" symbol, indicating they were ready to meet the challenge, just as early boxers threw their hats in the ring to demonstrate their willingness to fight. The top hat emblazoned with stars and stripes sailing through a circle was proudly painted on their airplane fuselages by the pilots. Their exploits were front-page news and followed closely in America. After World War I, Cook became one of our first transcontinental US Airmail pilots. He continued his pioneering efforts becoming Vice President of Curtiss Flying Service in Indiana. Cook was the first airport manager at the new Indianapolis Airport. Later, the airport was named to honor him after his death in a World War II military airplane crash. In 1976, the airport was renamed Indianapolis International Airport to reflect its many upgrades and improvements. In 2008, when a new terminal was built, both that building and the airport entrance road were named to honor Weir Cook.

Iowa: Sioux Gateway Airport Bud Day Field (KSUX) honors Medal of Honor winner, George Everette "Bud" Day, a local veteran Marine aviator, who flew in World War II, Korea, and Vietnam. Day is considered by many to be *the* most decorated US Military officer since Douglas MacArthur. While a POW in the infamous "Hanoi Hilton," Day was severely tortured, however, torture did not stop Bud Day from leading a resistance against the North Vietnamese guards. Colonel Day published several books, *Return with Honor and Duty, Honor, Country*. His life and service to America are honored at his home town airport.

Kansas: Wichita Dwight D. Eisenhower National Airport (KICT) honors World War II hero and United States President, Dwight David "Ike" Eisenhower. In the late 1930s, Eisenhower flew over 300 hours while stationed in the Philippines. Later, in 1939, at Ft. Lewis, WA, Eisenhower earned his FAA pilot's license. Knowledge of aviation was extremely important to his success as the World War II Supreme Commander of Allied Forces. During 1953 to 1961, as President, he experienced many aviation firsts: The first pilot to take the office, first President to travel aboard a plane designated "Air Force One," first President to fly on a helicopter, and first to fly in a Presidential jet. Eisenhower is photographed with one of the smaller Presidential airplanes, U-4B Aero Commander, with his Air Force pilot, Colonel William G. Draper. Wichita Dwight D. Eisenhower National Airport has a long and storied history. First as Wichita Municipal Airport, then Mid-Continent Airport, and now the largest airport in Kansas, the airport honors our nation's first aviator President.

Kentucky: Bowman Field Airport (KLOU) is a reliever airport for nearby Louisville International Airport. Bowman Field is Kentucky's first commercial airport and is one of our oldest continually operating commercial airfields. The airport was founded by Abram H. Bowman and Robert H. Gast, a World War I British Royal Flying Corps veteran. In 1919, the airport land was leased from the US Government. In 1921, the airfield opened. Aerial photography and other aviation businesses, along with the 465th Reserve Pursuit Squadron, populated the nascent field. By 1927, the airport hosted Charles Lindbergh and his Spirit of St. Louis to a huge crowd of spectators. During the 1930s Great Depression years, the federal Works Progress Administration (WPA) built the Art Deco-style terminal which attracted many local residents to visit their airport as a form of inexpensive entertainment. During the World War II years, Bowman Field became one of the nation's most important training bases described as "Air Base City." Bomber squadron trainees, the US Army Flight

Surgeon School, along with schools for medical technicians and flight nurses, populated the airport. In 1963, Bowman Field was the filming location for the epic James Bond movie, Gold Finger, for the Pussy Galore's Flying Circus segment. In 1988, the National Register of Historic Places designated the airport Administration Building, Curtiss Flying Service Hangar, and the Army Air Corps Hangar as historic treasurers. The landmark Bowman Field terminal is styled in aerodynamic Streamline Moderne.

Louisiana: Louis Armstrong New Orleans International Airport (KMSY), at only an average of 4.5 feet above sea level, is the world's second lowest lying international airport. The airport was originally named Moisant Field to honor daredevil aviator, John Moisant, who was killed in a 1910 airplane crash. The airport identifier, MSY, was derived from Moisant Stock Yards. As with many municipal airports during

World War II, it became an airbase. In 1946, commercial air service resumed. Over the years, terminal construction, expansions, and many airport improvements were completed. In 1961, the airport was renamed New Orleans International Airport for its expanding service. In 2001, in honor of the 100th anniversary of Louis Armstrong's birth, his hometown airport became Louis Armstrong New Orleans International Airport. African-American, Louis Daniel Armstrong, nicknamed "Satchmo," was an important American trumpeter, composer, and entertainer, who was an influential jazz figure with a stellar career spanning decades from the 1920s until his 1971 death. Armstrong's influence on popular music continues today.

Maine: Dewitt Field Old Town Municipal Airport and Seaplane Base (KOLD) honors local airport pioneer, Kenneth Dewitt, a Maine native born in 1908. DeWitt trained World War II pilots. In the early 1940s, he helped found and manage the airfield. He was an aviation business leader and airplane distributor. He died in 2008 at one hundred years old. This airport is unique with two paved runways and a seaplane base on the Penobscot River.

Maryland: Hagerstown Regional Airport Richard A. Henson Field (KHGR). This important airport honors aviation pioneer and Hagerstown native, Dick Henson. In 1928, the airport opened for public use on property owned by the Kreider-Reisner Aircraft Company. In 1933, the city purchased the airport, which was later sold to the Fairchild Aircraft Corporation for airplane manufacturing. During the years of World War II, Fairchild built PT-19 trainers shown in this photograph. Fairchild also built transport airplanes for the military. Aircraft production continued post-war until 1984. The airport was named Washington County Regional Airport until 1998 when it was renamed Hagerstown Regional Airport-Richard A. Henson Field. The airport slogan is "Your Local Connection to Hundreds of Destinations."

Massachusetts: Logan International Airport (KBOS) is officially named General Edward Lawrence Logan International Airport to honor Lawrence Logan, a Boston native, Harvard graduate, and Spanish-American War and World War I infantry commander. After World War I, Logan played a key role in reorganizing the Massachusetts National Guard. During his lifetime, he worked tirelessly for veterans' benefits, especially for high-risk military pilots. In 1943, after his death, the airport was renamed for his lifelong service. In 1923, it had been named Jeffery Field when it opened. In 1927, commercial service began from Boston to New York City. In 1952, Logan was one of the first US airport to connect with rapid transit. The airport expanded over the years to become one of the largest in the New England region in passenger and cargo volume. This photograph shows airport night operations.

Michigan: James Clements Municipal Airport (3CM) is a city-owned, public-use General Aviation Airport and Seaplane Base on the Saginaw River. In 1913, Lionel DeRemer owned the land and opened the first airport and flying school in the Saginaw Valley. Henry Dora was one of the first flying students. After Dora's return from World War I aviation military service, he bought a surplus Curtiss-JN-4 and barnstormed. Dora advocated for a permanent and modern airport. As with other airports, the Bay City Chamber of Commerce recognized the importance of airports in peacetime. In 1926, business and aviation leaders wanted to dedicate a new airport to the young men of Bay City who lost their lives in World War I. Wealthy local industrialist, William L. Clements, seized the opportunity to help the town and honor is son, naval aviator, James, who died in France during the war. Clements donated $10,000 (almost $150,000 today) for the construction of an airport. As other local leaders contributed, airport construction continued under the direction of Henry Dora. In 1928, the landing field and hangar were completed and officially dedicated with many planes using the new airport. In 1930, the administration building was completed. In 1982, it became part of the National Register of Historic Places.

Minnesota: South St. Paul Municipal Airport (KSGS) also known as Richard E. Fleming Field or Fleming Field is named for Saint Paul native, World War II United States Marine Corps aviator, Medal of Honor recipient, Richard E. Fleming, who bravely flew in the epic Battle of Midway. Only ten days after America entered World War II, Fleming piloted his Vought SB2U Vindicator with his squadron from Pearl Harbor to Midway Island. On June 5, 1942, after heavy combat operations, at only age twenty-four, his airplane was hit with heavy flak, caught fire, and crashed into the sea with Fleming still at the controls. His Medal of Honor citation reads in part, "For extraordinary heroism and conspicuous gallantry above and beyond the call of duty."

Mississippi: Meridian Regional Airport (KMEI) at Key Field is a joint-use civil/military airfield. Key Field is home to Mississippi's longest public-use runway of 10,003 feet. In 1928, the airport was established. By November, 1930, it opened with the terminal, hangar, power station, and a graded, packed dirt runway. Fred and Al Key opened Key Brothers Flying School. They operated their school and co-managed the new airport. The brothers sold commercial airline tickets, operated the terminal, and handled airmail delivery schedules. With the hard economic times of the Great Depression years, city leaders considered abandoning the airport because airmail deliveries slowed and few could afford to fly on the airliners or take flying lessons. Still, maintenance funds were needed for daily operations and safety. Undaunted, the Key brothers devised a plan to keep their beloved airport open. They hoped that if they broke the twenty-three-day flight endurance record, they would focus worldwide attention on Meridian Airport. The Key brothers, along with local inventor, A. D. Hunter, and mechanic, James Keeton, invented an improved air-to-air refueling system. If fuel spilled down from above on the airplane engine, it would catch fire. Their ingenious system consisted of a valve on the end of the fuel nozzle, which was opened by a probe in the neck of the fuel tank. This new valve would not allow fuel to flow unless it was inserted into the fuel tank. During refueling, if the nozzle were removed from the tank, the fuel would automatically stop flowing. Later, the US Army adopted their new invention. Another challenge for the brothers was regular engine maintenance during the flight to keep the small, five-cylinder motor humming. The problem was solved by inventing a catwalk so Fred could walk out and work on the engine while airborne. Engine oil came from a special reserve tank. Donations and local support helped fund this mission impossible. By June 4, 1935, the Key brothers and the world were ready. They borrowed a Curtiss Robin monoplane named "Ole Miss." She slowly climbed above Meridian. For the next twenty-seven days, the Keys flew over Meridian. For food and other supplies, they used a similar airplane which dropped the items to the brothers on the end of a rope, as well as supply fuel via a long flexible tube. The landing was July 1 to a crowd estimated at 40,000 people for this historic aviation event. The Keys had flown an estimated 52,320 miles over their community and used more than 6,000 gallons of gasoline. Their feat was headline news around the world. The Keys and their intrepid band of aviation brothers and sisters had saved their airport. Their non-stop endurance flight lasted 653 hours and 34 minutes. "Ole Miss" is permanently displayed in the National Air and Space Museum in Washington, D. C. Because of their Herculean efforts, their home airport was renamed Key Field in honor of the brothers. But, wait! There is even more to the Key brothers' story. They also had distinguished World War II aviation service in the Pacific, earning even more recognition. Today, these early aviation pioneers are honored at Key Field. The hangar and offices are listed on the National Register of Historic Places.

Missouri: St. Louis Lambert International Airport (KSTL) is named in honor of Albert Bond Lambert, early promoter of Midwest air travel. In 1911, Lambert learned to fly with the Wright Brothers. He served in World War I reaching the rank of Army Major. In 1920, when he returned to St. Louis, Major Lambert partnered with the Missouri Aeronautical Society to lease land for a St. Louis airfield. At his own expense, Lambert cleared the land, graded and drained it, built a hangar, paid the land lease, and offered the site for free for aviation purposes. World War I veterans, William and Frank Robertson, accepted this generous offer and opened what became known as St. Louis Flying Field. In 1923, the newly formed Missouri National Guard 110th Observation Squadron formed on the field. Lambert was responsible for organizing the highly successful 1923 International Air Races in St. Louis. Soon after, as a reward for his tireless efforts, Lambert St. Louis Flying Field was christened. Attending the Air Races was young pilot, Charles Lindbergh, who liked what he saw. Lindbergh stayed on at Lambert as a flight instructor. When the airport land lease expired in 1925, Lambert bought the property. That same year, the US Post Office awarded Robertson the Chicago-St. Louis airmail service contract with Lindbergh as the chief pilot. While flying the mail, Lindbergh decided to seek the Orteig Prize for the first non-stop flight between New York and Paris.

Major Lambert and other air-minded St. Louis citizens agreed to support him. The rest, as they say, is aviation history.

Montana: Bert Mooney Airport (KBTM) named in 1972 to honor Butte aviation pioneer, Bert Mooney, who began flying in 1919. He founded Butte Aero Sales at the airfield. Later, he became the chief pilot for Western Air Express (Western Airlines). In 1935, he was the first to fly mail into Yellowstone National Park. In 1926, the airport opened as Butte Municipal. In 1937, the New Deal Federal Emergency Relief Administration and Works Progress Administration contributed to improving the municipal airport. In 1960 to 1972, the airport was known as Silver Bow County Airport.

Nebraska: Western Nebraska Regional Airport William B. Heilig Field (KBFF). In 1928, Airmail service began. By 1934,

Scottsbluff was firmly established on that circuit which grew into today's airport. During World War II, the airport became Scottsbluff Army Airfield. Instruction for B-17-Flying Fortress and B-24-Liberator crews was conducted there. In 1947, the city of Scottsbluff resumed airport ownership. William B. Heilig, who served as a World War II US Army Air Corps flight instructor, became airport manager. He continued to promote the airport's post-war growth. In 1993, Heilig was inducted into the Nebraska Aviation Hall of Fame. The new terminal building honors Scottsbluff Citizen of the Century, former city councilman, mayor, and long-serving Airport Authority leader, Donald E. Overman.

Nevada: Elko Regional Airport J.C. Harris Field (KEKO), formerly Elko Municipal Airport, is named for Jess C. Harris, an US Airmail Service mechanic from 1920-27. He moved to Elko to serve twelve years on the police force. In 1931, he earned a pilot license. From 1940-45, Harris flew as a Lockheed test pilot. He returned to Elko as undersheriff until he was elected sheriff in 1950. Elected six times, he became known as Nevada's "Flying Sheriff," building up 13,000 hours of flight time. Elko Regional Airport is one of the earliest US airports. The airport was a waypoint on the very first transcontinental airmail route. In March 1919, aviation began in Elko when the US Post Office requested the town create a rudimentary airfield on the former Southern Pacific Railroad stockyards. That original site continues to serve Elko as an airport. Surplus World War I canvass hangars were used to house the very first airplanes. The US Army was the first to fly into Elko and was enthusiastically embraced by local citizens who were captured by the allure of this modern form of transportation. In 1920, locals funded a flight service station constructed on the airport. By 1924, Elko became a significant way point for east-west aviation traffic. In 1924, the Beacon Hill beacon provided pilots with visual navigation from a hundred nautical miles away. Elko was a benefactor of early Federal aviation development, serving as a location for lighted air beacons that provided navigational aids for night flying on Air Route #1.

New Hampshire: Nashua Airport at Boire Field (KASH) was named in 1943 to honor Ensign Paul Boire, Nashua's first World War II casualty. The airport dates back to 1934, when the city of Nashua bought a small existing airport, which lacked a hangar and had only a grass runway. Over the next several years, Nashua, with federal help, paved the runway and built airport buildings. The hangar was constructed from bricks salvaged from a factory burned in the 1930 Crown Hill Fire. Today the airport slogan is "Your Gateway to Nashua and the World."

New Jersey: Many important airports are based in the state. One particular airport, however, serves as a reminder of how often and quickly an airport can be closed. On September 30, 2006, the historic Bader Field, also known as Atlantic City Municipal Airport, was permanently closed by the city. In 1910, it opened and was named for the former Atlantic City Mayor, Edward L. Bader, who championed the purchase of the land for the airport. In 1911, passenger service was authorized. It was the very first US municipal airport with facilities for both land-based airplanes and seaplanes. The first known usage of the term "airport" was coined in a 1919 newspaper article about Bader Field. In 1941, Bader Field was the location of the founding of the Civil Air Patrol. Because residential and casino developers viewed Bader Field land as a prime development site, Bader Field closed, joining a long list of fine airports fallen prey to developers.

New Mexico: Lea County–Zip Franklin Memorial Airport (E06) is also known as Lovington Airport. It is named for aviator, Oliver Gene "Zip" Franklin. Born in 1919 in Artesia, New Mexico, Zip Franklin purchased his first airplane at age 16, a 1929 "Doyle Special" a.k.a. the O-3 Oriole. This began his love affair with flying. He served in the US Army during World War II, returning home to Lovington. Soon, he became known as the "original flying rancher," flying the thirty miles between his farm and ranch near Lovington. Zip's descendants are the long-running Franklin's Flying Circus family with over fifty years of celebrated aerobatics performances. While Jimmy Franklin is recognized as the founder, his son, Kyle, is the major force in the Franklin's Flying Circus today. Their passion for flight came from Zip Franklin. In the photograph, Kyle Franklin strikes a pose during a wing walking routine on top of a jet-powered Waco bi-plane, flown by his father, Jimmy, during a 2005 Air Show.

New York: Many New York airports pay tribute to aviation and national leaders. John F. Kennedy International Airport (KJFK) honors the former US President. LaGuardia Airport (KLGA) recognizes former New York City Mayor, Fiorello LaGuardia. Earlier, that location was the historic Glenn H. Curtiss Airport. A lessor known airport is Greater Binghamton Airport Edwin A. Link Field (KBGM), which was originally Broome County Airport. This airport developed because of difficult night flying operations in the New York City area. In 1951, longer and crosswind runways were expanded and constructed. In early 1980s, the field was renamed in honor of Edwin A. Link, the Binghamton inventor of the Link Trainer. In the 1990s, the airport name changed to Binghamton Regional, and, then in 2003, Greater Binghamton Airport. The addition of Link's name honors his incredible aviation-training simulator.

Link Trainers, also called "Bluebox" pilot trainers, were a series of flight simulators produced between early 1930s to early 1950s by Binghamton's Link Aviation Devices. Founded in 1929 by Edwin "Ed" Link, the Link trainers provided a safe, new way to teach instrument flying to more than 500,000 American pilots and many others across the globe. Given Historic Mechanical Engineering Landmark status by the prestigious American Society of Mechanical Engineers, the Link Trainer and its inventor live on through this airport.

North Dakota: Mercer County Regional Airport Al Joersz Field (KHZE) honors Hazen native and decorated combat pilot, Major General Eldon (Al) Joersz. A former Vietnam-era Air Force pilot and Wing Commander, Joersz was chosen as a flight instructor for the SR-71, long-range, high-altitude, strategic reconnaissance aircraft nicknamed "Blackbird" and "Habu." On July 28, 1976, Joersz jointly set the World Air Speed record flying over 2,193 miles per hour, making the North Dakota aviator one of the "world's fastest pilots."

Ohio: In 2003, Congress officially declared Ohio as the "birthplace of aviation" because Dayton was the home of Wilbur and Orville Wright, who are credited with inventing and flying the first heavier-than-air aircraft.

John Glenn Columbus International Airport (KCMH) honors our first American to orbit Planet Earth, Ohio's former US Senator (1974-1999), the late John Glenn. In 1959, Glenn became one of the original Mercury Seven military pilots selected as America's first astronauts. On February 20, 1962, John Glenn donned his silver pressure suit, climbed into Friendship 7 spaceship launched by a Mercury Atlas rocket to orbit the Earth.

Another Ohio airport honoring an aviation legend is Rickenbacker International Airport (KLCK). In 1974, it was named to honor Columbus native, Eddie Rickenbacker. A highly acclaimed World War I Ace with twenty-six aerial victories that earned Rickenbacker the Medal of Honor. In fact, he earned the most awards for valor by an American during that war. Before the war, he was a race car driver and automotive designer. He innately understood mechanical parts and engine repair. His life story is like a Hollywood movie where through talent and hard work, our hero become an aviation legend. He was a pioneer of civilian air transportation as well. As the long-time leaders of Eastern airlines, Eddie Rickenbacker said, "Aviation is proof that given the will, we have the capacity to achieve the impossible." Airports and aviation prove daily that Rickenbacker was correct. Rickenbacker International Airport has a long history, too. In June 1942, the airport opened as Lockbourne Army Airfield. It was used for basic pilot training. It provided B-17 flight training to the Women Airforce Service Pilots (WASP), too. In later years, the Tuskegee Airman served there. The Department of the Air Force redesignated Lockbourne Air Force Base to Rickenbacker Air Force Base. Today this legendary airport is a joint-use civil/ military airport honoring a true American aviation hero.

Oklahoma: Wiley Post Airport (KPWA). Wiley Post became enamored with planes as a youth and dreamed of becoming a pilot. In 1913, he had his first airplane flight at the County Fair in Lawton, Oklahoma. Later, when a barnstorming troop came to Oklahoma, Post filled in for an injured skydiver. Post began work in the oil fields to earn enough money to buy his own plane. His plans were nearly derailed when he lost an eye in a work-related accident. As a result, Post initially had trouble with depth perception, but ultimately he trained himself to gauge distances accurately with only one eye. Post took the $1,800 accident compensation to buy his first airplane. In that airplane, he gave flying lessons, flew oilmen to their rigs, and barnstormed on the weekends. In 1928, Post became the personal pilot to F.C. Hall, an Oklahoma oilman. It was in Hall's Lockheed Vega, the "Winnie Mae," that Post won the 1930 National Air Race from Los Angeles to Chicago. The first of many accomplishments in this famous aircraft. On June 23, 1931, he and Australian navigator, Harold Gatty, took off from Roosevelt Field in Long Island, with the goal of breaking the record for flying around the world. Eight days, fifteen hours, and fifty-one minutes later, the pair touched down again at Roosevelt Field, after circling the globe and smashing the previous record of twenty days and four hours. The pair became instant worldwide heroes. In 1932, by an Act of Congress, Post received the Distinguished Flying Cross. In that same year, he won the Collier Trophy. In 1934, he won the Gold Medal of Belgium and the International Harmon Trophy. Post was given two, New York City ticker-tape parades and the keys to the City. He was honored twice at the White House by two Presidents—Herbert Hoover and Franklin Delano Roosevelt. From his record-breaking flights to his innovations and explorations, Wiley Post made many vital contributions that advanced the science and theory of flight. Post set numerous altitude records and discovered the jet stream. Wiley Post is one our most celebrated pilots in our aviation history.

Pennsylvania: Arnold Palmer Regional Airport (KLBE) in Latrobe honors America's golfing legend and accomplished pilot, Arnold Palmer. Born in Youngstown and raised close to the Latrobe airport, as a young boy, he would make balsawood airplane models to show the pilots at the old airport terminal building. A family friend gave him his first airplane ride in a vintage Piper Cub. Palmer is regarded as one of the greatest and most charismatic players in professional golf history. Palmer's legacy spanned six decades. Arnie Palmer won the Masters Golf Tournament four times. As his professional golfing career grew, along with his family, Palmer traded the highway for the Latrobe airport runway. In 1955, he began flight lessons in a Cessna 172, eventually earning his private, instrument, and multi-engine ratings. Palmer served on the airport board. Over the years, he encouraged airport improvements and expansion, resulting in Regional airport status. Palmer flew over 18,000 hours at the controls of his own planes. Over the years, Arnie owned and flew many planes to include Aero Commanders, Cessna Citations, and a Rockwell Jet Commander. On May 19, 1976, flying his Lear 36, he set a world record for circumnavigating the globe. In 1999, his home airport was named in his honor.

Rhode Island: T.F. Green International Airport (KPVD), a.k.a. Green Airport, is officially named Theodore Francis Green Memorial State Airport, honoring former Rhode Island Governor and Senator. In 1931, the airport was dedicated as Hillsgrove State Airport, making it the first state-owned airport in the United States. In 1933, the Rhode Island State Airport Terminal was built. In 1938, the airport was named for T. F. Green, who had just been elected Senator two years earlier. During 1942 to 1945, the airport was taken over by the Army

Air Corps for flight training. Runways were lengthened. When the airport returned to civil use, improvements continued. The most recent was the 1996 renovated main terminal named for another former governor. Bruce Sundlun. In 2018, the state legislature was petitioned to change the name to Rhode Island International Airport to reflect the mission and service area.

South Carolina: Jim Hamilton-L.B. Owens Airport (KCUB) honors former airport manager, Jim Hamilton. When the airport was originally dedicated in 1930, it was named Columbia Municipal Airport. The historic Curtiss-Wright Hangar was the first permanent structure in those early days. In 1932, Eastern Air Transport began airmail and passenger service. During World War II, the airport was used as a training field for Army Air Corps reconnaissance and observation pilots, while still remaining open for civil commercial service. After the war, the airport was renamed Owens Field for Columbia Mayor, Lawrence B. Owens, one the most ardent supporters of a municipal airport. In 1947, the US Air Force released its former World War II base to Lexington County. That became

Columbia Metropolitan Airport (KCAE) and the main commercial air service airport. Today, Jim Hamilton-L.B. Owens Airport provides safe and efficient facilities in support of General and Business Aviation. Another mission is to serve as a reliever airport for the Columbia Metropolitan Airport.

South Dakota: Sioux Falls Regional Airport-Joe Foss Field (KFSD) is named for famed US Marine Aviator, Joseph Jacob "Joe" Foss. Joe was inspired to fly watching Charles Lindbergh performing at a local air show. During World War II as a fighter pilot, he became the leading Ace of the Marine Corps, matching the record of twenty-six kills held by America's top World War I Ace, Eddie Rickenbacker. Foss was accorded the honor of becoming America's First World War II "Ace-of-Aces." Foss was recognized with the Medal of Honor for his aerial combat during the Guadalcanal Campaign. After World War II, Foss returned home. In 1946, he commanded the South Dakota Air National Guard. After retiring as a Brigadier General from his

Air Guard leadership, Joe Foss went on to serve as Governor from 1955 to 1959. He became the first Commissioner of the National Football League, and an author of several military aviation books, including Top Guns: America's Fighter Aces Tell their Stories. The airport which honors him was established in 1937. In 1942, the Sioux Falls airport was converted to national defense with the establishment of a radio operator training facility, which trained about 40,000 skilled radio operators. Today, this important airport is the largest in South Dakota.

Tennessee: McKellar-Sipes Regional Airport (KMKL) was established by and originally named in memory of Kenneth Douglas McKellar, Tennessee's longtime US Senator. McKellar convinced the federal Civil Works Administration to acquire the property and construct runways and buildings during the winter of 1933-34. Later in the 1930s, the Works Project Administration (WPA) expanded the airport runways and constructed additional buildings. During World War II, the airport was leased by the US Army Air Corps for wartime flight training. Air cadets flew PT-17 Stearman biplanes as the primary trainer. Also, Fairchild PT-19 and other airplanes were added to the training fleet. In 1945, the air base was declared surplus and became a civil airport again. In the 1970s, the airport name was amended to also honor, Major Robert Ray "Buster" Sipes, a stellar US Air Force test pilot from Jackson, who was killed in England in a 1969 RF 101 Voodoo jet fighter crash. Today, the Tennessee Army National Guard UH-60 Blackhawk helicopters are stationed at the McKellar-Sipes Regional Airport.

Texas: George Bush Intercontinental Airport (KIAH) honors George Herbert Walker Bush, our nation's 41st President and distinguished World War II Naval Aviator. The airport is relatively new, planned in early 1957 by a group of Houston business leaders. In 1969, the airport officially opened as Houston Intercontinental Airport. It grew into a major airline hub and required additional terminal construction over the years. In 1997, it was renamed George Bush Intercontinental Airport. The backstory of naval aviator, George Bush, is remarkable. Shortly after the December 7, 1941 Japanese Pearl Harbor attack, Bush enlisted in the Navy on his eighteenth birthday. Before age nineteen, he became one of their youngest aviators. He was assigned to fly torpedo bombers off an aircraft carrier in the Pacific. On September 2, 1944, at dawn, piloting his Grumman TBM Avenger, Bush and his crew flew a mission to destroy a heavily defended Japanese communications and supply station. His plane was hit with flak. The engine caught fire. Choking on smoke in the cockpit, twenty-year-old Bush piloted the plane to drop his payload on the radio tower, completing the mission. He told his crew members to parachute, while he would fly the plane as long as he could. Plane ablaze, he finally parachuted out. The plane crashed in the ocean. He was able to inflate a raft and survive a strafing attack by enemy fighters. Later, he was rescued by the USS Finback submarine. Bush flew fifty-eight combat missions, earning the Distinguished Flying Cross. After World War II was over, Bush pursued successful business and political careers. This major airport memorializes the stellar accomplishments of George Herbert Walker Bush.

Utah: Hill Air Force Base (KHIF) honors US Army Air Corps Major Ployer Peter Hill, who died in 1935 testing NX13372, the original Boeing Model prototype of the B-17 Flying Fortress bomber. He was the Chief of the Flying Branch. Hill Air Force Base traces its origins to the US Army's Airmail "experiment" of 1934 where surveys were done to establish a suitable location for a permanent western terminus of the airmail route. In 1939,

Congress appropriated $8,000,000 (almost $150,000,000 today) for the construction of the Ogden Air Depot. On November 7, 1940, Hill Field officially opened. With America's entry into World War II, Hill Field quickly grew with round-the-clock maintenance, supply, and repair of battle-worn airplanes as the B-17, B-24, B-29, P-40, P-47 and others. All were sent to Hill for structural repairs, engine overhauls, anything to keep them flying. Thousands of warplanes were returned to combat. On February 5, 1947, Hill Field became Hill Air Force Base. Hill AFB played a significant role again during the Korean War. During the Vietnam War, maintenance support for various kinds of jet warplanes as the F-4 Phantom were part of the modern mission. Today, even more modern military aircraft and air combat missile systems and air-to-ground rockets are included in Hill Air Force Base national security mission. On April 29, 2019, airman from the 729th Air Control Squadron return home to Hill AFB, after seven long months of Middle East deployment.

Vermont: Hartness State Airport (KVSF) is Vermont's first officially approved airport. In 1916, at the age of fifty-five, James Hartness, head of Springfield Tool & Die and an inventor-engineer, earned a pilot's license. By 1919, he purchased land to create the Springfield Landing Field airport. By 1921, the Harkness Flying School opened. That same year, Harkness was elected Governor of Vermont. Hartness organized the official visit of Charles Lindbergh as part of the Guggenheim tour to forty-eight states and ninety-two cities from July 20 to October 23, 1927. Even before Charles Lindbergh took off for Paris on that historic May 20 flight, aviation enthusiast, Harry Guggenheim, told Lindbergh to contact him after Lindbergh landed in Paris. Later, Guggenheim admitted he did not think Lindbergh would survive the attempt across the Atlantic Ocean solo because several had already perished trying. Well, after Lindbergh returned to America, he remembered the multi-millionaire's offer to promote aviation. It was a partnership which had profound impact on American aviation and airports. The Guggenheim Fund sponsored Lindbergh and the Spirit of St. Louis on the three-month nationwide tour. Lindbergh gave 147 speeches about the importance of aviation to America and rode 1,290 miles in parades as part of the enormous celebration. Literally millions of Americans saw Lindbergh and the Spirit of St. Louis. Airmail usage exploded as a result. Communities began to construct and expand landing fields into airports.

Virginia: Lynchburg Regional Airport also known as Preston Glenn Field (KLYH) opened in 1931. Originally named Preston Glenn Airport to honor Lynchburg native, Lt. Preston Glenn, who was the only local World War I aviator to perish overseas. Glenn grew up in Lynchburg where he served in the local National Guard unit called the "Musketeers." In 1917, he enlisted in the Aviation Section, training as a fighter pilot in France. During aerial combat, he was shot down by a German plane. Although badly wounded, he was taken to a German Prisoner of War camp where he died from his wounds. Over the years, the airport has grown. In 1992, a new terminal opened and the new regional service is reflected in the airport name. The airport plays a key role in regional growth, serving as a convenient global gateway for the areas' international corporations, manufacturing, research, and educational leaders.

Washington: Snohomish County Airport–Paine Field Airport (KPAE) was constructed in 1936 as a Works Progress Administration (WPA) project. It is named in honor of Lieutenant Topliff Olin Paine, Everett native and a pilot in the Army Air Corps, and, later, an Airmail Service pilot. Paine was considered one of the top fliers in the US Airmail Service Western Division. He received nationwide recognition for flying feats on the treacherous Rock Springs WY to Salt Lake City UT route which he started. With America's World War II entry, the protection of Bremerton Shipyards and the Boeing B-17 and B-29 aircraft plant was paramount. The Army Air Corps manned the airfield from 1941–1946 and significantly improved the airport. In 1946, the facility was returned to

Snohomish County. Then, in 1951, when the Korean War again demonstrated the important strategic location, the name was changed to Paine Air Force Base. The airport shared military and civil use which allowed for the development of an industrial airpark. Later, Boeing constructed a B-747 assembly plant on the airport. Today, this historic airfield offers an array of diverse aviation industry services.

West Virginia: Yeager Airport (KCRW) in Charleston is named for legendary World War II, Korean, and Vietnam War aviator, and famed test pilot, Charles E. "Chuck" Yeager. At the start of World War II, Yeager enlisted as an aircraft mechanic. In just a few months, he was selected for military pilot training. With incredible visual acuity and a natural gift for flying, he excelled. On October 12, 1944, flying P-51 Mustangs in combat in Europe, he became an Ace in one day by downing five enemy aircraft in a single mission. Officially, by wars' end, he logged sixty-four combat missions and more official victories to add to his Ace credentials. All of these incredible actions were despite having his planes shot down several times, evading the enemy, and heroically carrying a wounded B-24 navigator on his back over the Pyrenees to escape the enemy.

Even with his own combat wounds, he convinced the military leadership that he should keep flying and fighting. After World War II, he was a natural selection for the new military test pilot program. On October 14, 1947, he strapped his compact body into a rocket-powered experimental aircraft. Yeager reached Mach 1 and broke the sound barrier at an altitude of 45,000 feet in his Bell X-1, named Glamorous Glennis for his wife. In 1985, his home state renamed the former Kanawha airport for aviation icon, Brigadier General Chuck Yeager.

Wisconsin: Austin Straubel International Airport (KGRB) honors Austin Straubel, Green Bay native from an historic pioneer family. Straubel was the first Brown County World War II aviator to lose his life. Flying in the Pacific, Major Straubel commanded several squadrons. He earned the Distinguished Flying Cross for his combat flying. On February 3, 1942, he was killed. On March 20, 1946, when the new Brown County airport opened, it was named in his honor. In 2016, as the airport and its services have grown, the airport was officially renamed Green Bay Austin Straubel International Airport.

Wittman Regional Airport (KOSH) is a vibrant gateway to Wisconsin and a legacy center of aeronautical innovation. Named for Steve Wittman, pioneer air racer and aircraft designer, it was originally named Winnebago County Airport. The Spirit of Aviation burns brightly at the annual July Experimental Aircraft Association EAA AirVenture known as "Oshkosh." Earlier, other Wisconsin airports hosted the annual EAA gathering of aviation enthusiasts. By 1969, it was clear a permanent and larger location was needed. With strong local support, Oshkosh was a natural location. Volunteers spent months erecting additional infrastructure and buildings to host the annual "EAA Gathering of Eagles." By 1998, EAA AirVenture Oshkosh became the name. Now, with over 10,000 airplanes, 600,000 aviation visitors, volunteers, exhibitors, and aviation leaders in attendance at this annual extravaganza, world-class status is associated with this annual signature aviation event. AirVenture is so flooded with transient aircraft that the Oshkosh control tower becomes the "World's Busiest!"

Wyoming: Ralph Wenz Field Airport (KPNA) is named for pioneer aviator and airmail pilot, US Marine Staff Sergeant Ralph Wenz. On December 21, 1943, Wenz and his B-24 Liberator crew members crashed in the Alaskan wilderness. Wenz first learned to fly in Wyoming. As an experienced pilot, he was assigned to instruct military pilots in the hazards of flying in sub-zero weather, testing new procedures and equipment in fog and icing conditions. In the 1940s, the Pinedale airport named in his memory had humble beginnings as a grass landing strip. In the 1950s, the first paved runway appeared. In 1968, the runway was lengthened with money raised by local business leaders. Over the years, the airport has expanded. In 2008, a longer 8,900 foot runway allows for more efficient aircraft operations.

Remember, a mile of highway takes you just a mile. A mile of runway connects you to the world.

EXPLORE MORE

RESOURCES

Books:

- Bednarek, Janet R. Airports, Cities, and the Jet Age: US Airports Since 1945, New York, NY: Palgrave Macmillan, 2016.

- Bubb, Daniel K. Landing in Las Vegas: Commercial Aviation and the Making of a Tourist City. Reno NV: University of Nevada Press, 2012.

- Bloom, Nicholas Dagen. The Metropolitan Airport: JFK International and modern New York, Phildelphia, PA: University of Pennsylvania Press, 2015.

- Grant, R.G. Flight: The Complete History of Aviation. New York, NY: DK Publishing, 2017.

- Marquez, Victor. Landside/Airside: Why Airports Are The Way They Area, New York, NY: Palgrave Macmillan, 2019.

- Martin, Isabel. An Airport Field Trip. North Mankato, MN: Capstone Press, 2015.

- Moyle, Terry. Art Deco Airports: Airports of Dreams from 1920s & 1930s. London, England: New Holland Publishers, 2015.

- Price, Jeffrey C., Jeffrey S. Forrest, Shahn G. Sederberg. Denver Airport: From Stapleton to DIA, Charleston, SC: Arcadia Publishing, 2018. (Images of Aviation Series extensive library of airport history books)

- Talbott, Stanley & Michael E. Kassel. Wyoming Airmail Pioneers. Charleston SC: The History Press, 2017.

- The Epic of Flight 23 Volume Set. Chicago, IL: Time-Life Books, 1981.

Aviation Career Information

- Aviation Careers: Jobs, Salaries & Educational Requirements www.thebestschools.org/careers/aviation-careers/

- How to Work in the Aviation Field www.learnhowtobecome.org/science-technology-careers/aviation/

- Popular Aviation Careers www.avjobs.com/careers/

- On-line Aviation Organizations And Resources

- Aircraft Owners & Pilots Association www.aopa.org

- Air Line Pilots Association www.ALPA.org

- Air Traffic Control Association www.ATCA.org

- American Association of Airport Executives www.aaae.org

- Association of Flight Attendants-CWA www.afacwa.org

- Experimental Aircraft Association-EAA Young Eagles Program www.eaa.org

- Helicopter Association International www.rotor.org

- Living with Your Airplane Association www.livingwithyourplane.com

- National Air Transportation Association www.NATA.aero

- National Association of State Aviation Officials www.nasao.org

- National Business Aviation Association www.NBAA.org

- Professional Aviation Maintenance Association www.PAMA.org

- Recreational Aviation Foundation www.theRAF.org

- Seaplane Pilots Association www.seaplanepilotsassociation.org

- Soaring Society of America www.ssa.org

- University Aviation Association www.uaa.aero

- Women in Aviation International www.wai.org

PHOTO CREDITS

Page 27: LOC
Page 29: US Postal Service
Page 32: LOC
Page 33: LOC
Page 34: CC0
Page 35: Wikimedia.org
Page 36: LOC
Page 38: Wikimedia.org/Mlickliter
Page 39: LOC
Page 40: LOC
Page 41: LOC
Page 42: LOC
Page 44: LOC
Page 45: LOC
Page 47: Dennis Heap/Rocky Mountain Airways
Page 48: Crista Worthy
Page 49 top: LOC
Page 49 bottom: Courtesy Denver International Airport
Page 51: Penny Rafferty Hamilton
Page 52 top: Wikimedia.org
Page 52 bottom: Randy Coller
Page 53: LOC
Page 54 top: Penny Rafferty Hamilton
Page 54 bottom: Penny Rafferty Hamilton
Page 55 top: Penny Rafferty Hamilton
Page 55 bottom: North Dakota Aeronautics Commission
Page 56 top: Penny Rafferty Hamilton
Page 56 bottom: Penny Rafferty Hamilton
Page 57 top: Penny Rafferty Hamilton
Page 57 bottom: Penny Rafferty Hamilton
Page 58 top: Jon Simmers/Bismarck Aero Center
Page 58 bottom: Penny Rafferty Hamilton
Page 59 top: CC0/Matthew Turner
Page 59 bottom: Courtesy Denver International Airport
Page 60 top: Courtesy Denver International Airport
Page 60 bottom: Penny Rafferty Hamilton
Page 64 Penny Rafferty Hamilton
Page 65 Courtesy Denver International Airport
Page 66 top: Aviation Alphabet chart
Page 66 bottom: Penny Rafferty Hamilton
Page 67: Jon Simmers/Bismarck Aero Center
Page 68: NOTAM FAA
Page 69: Penny Rafferty Hamilton
Page 71: Courtesy Denver International Airport
Page 72 top: Jon Simmers/Bismarck Aero Center
Page 72 bottom: CC0
Page 73 top: Microsoft clip art
Page 73 bottom: Courtesy Denver International Airport
Page 74 top: Courtesy Denver International Airport
Page 74 bottom: Jon Simmers/Bismarck Aero Center
Page 75 top: Courtesy Denver International Airport
Page 75 bottom: Courtesy Denver International Airport

Page 76 top: Courtesy Denver International Airport
Page 76 bottom: Penny Rafferty Hamilton
Page 77: LOC
Page 78: Wikimedia.org
Page 79: Prescott Regional Airport Authority
Page 80: City of Bentonville
Page 81 top: Courtesy Charles M. Schulz–Sonoma County Airport
    (KSTS)
Page 81 bottom: LOC
Page 82: Emily Warner Field Aviation Museum
Page 83: Connecticut Airport Authority
Page 84 top: US Air Force photo/Roland Balik
Page 84 bottom: stpete.org
Page 85: athensairport.net
Page 86 Owen Miyamoto photographer
Page 87: Steven Kjergaard Airport Director (KCOE)
Page 88: LOC
Page 89: Chuck Choi/Courtesy of HOK
Page 90: US Air Force archive photograph
Page 91: Air Force Museum archive
Page 92: Works Progress Administration archive
Page 93: LOC
Page 94: Mary Gibouleau
Page 95: NASA archive
Page 96: Wikimedia.org
Page 97: Doug Dodge/Fly 3CM
Page 98: Richard E. Fleming Field
Page 99 Wikimedia
Page 101: CC0
Page 102 top: Bert Mooney Airport (KBTM)
Page 102 bottom: Western Nebraska Regional Airport
Page 103: Wikimedia.org
Page 104: Wikimedia.org/Mark Buckawicki
Page 105: Abandoned & Little Known Airfields www.airfields-free-
    man.com
Page 106: US Navy photo/Daniel McLain
Page 107: Wikimedia Commons/Tony Speer
Page 108: North Dakota Aeronautics Commission
Page 109: NASA archive
Page 110: Sixflashphoto
Page 111: LOC
Page 112: Westmoreland County Airport Authority
Page 113: Wikimedia.org
Page 114: Eagle Aviation, Inc.
Page 115: Air National Guard archive
Page 116: USAF photo of F-101A
Page 117: LOC
Page 118: USAF photo/R. Nial Bradshaw
Page 119: wikicommons.org/Ynsalh
Page 120: City of Lynchburg
Page 121: Wikicommons.org
Page 122: Central West Virginia Airport Authority

Page 123: Green Bay Austin Straubel Intl. Airport
Page 124: Kim Stevens
Page 125: USAF archival photograph
Page 126: North Dakota Aeronautics Commission
Page 127: CC0
Page 129: Ann Stricklin
Page 147: Colorado Women's Hall of Fame

INDEX

A

B

C

D

E

F

G

H

L

M

N

O

P

Q

R

S

T

W

ACKNOWLEDGMENTS

Any important project depends upon a team. *America's Amazing Airports* has a large aviation community of support. Starting with Gordon Page, founder of the Spirit of Flight Foundation, and Kim Peticolas for design and publishing assistance.

Other contributions were made by: Phil Boyer, Colorado Aeronautics Division, Colorado Aviation Historical Society, Colorado Soaring Association-especially Neil R. Van Lieu and Curt Cole, Ray Hawkins-Colorado Pilots Association Seaplane Liaison, Mary Gibouleau, Grand County Library District-Granby Branch, Dennis Heap, Idaho Aviation Association-Crista Worthy, Kip McClain, Kopy Kat Office-Gillian Butler, Mike McHugh-North Dakota Aeronautics Commission, Lauren Gompertz Norby, Shahn Sederberg, Sandy Shevers and Sporty's Pilot Shop staff, Jon Simmers-Bismarck Aero Center, Aaron Skinner, Diana Smith-Beatrice Airport, State Aviation Journal-Kim Stevens, Ann Stricklin, Crystal Tafoya, Tavares City, Mark Twombly-Water Flying Magazine, David Ulane, Petra Videriksen, and Kim Weeks at Avlite Systems. A sincere "thank you" to the many other airport leaders listed in the photo credits. We all owe gratitude to America's aviation pioneers and airport professionals, who created and maintain our world-class aviation system.

Because our brains process photo images much faster than text, this quick flight through our airport history relies heavily on archival images and photographs. In addition to the author's and donated photographs, other sources were Library of Congress as LOC, Creative Commons as CC0, Denver International Airport, and Wikimedia.org.

We hope you enjoy reading about airport history as much as we delighted in researching and writing it for you. Please explore aviation career opportunities, too. Join us in the wonderful world of airports and aviation.

ABOUT THE AUTHOR

Dr. Hamilton began her newspaper and photography career in 1982. She continues to publish in many and varied publications on aviation, health, and women's history. She has won several national and state business and writing awards, including recognition from the US Small Business Administration, National Association of State Aviation Officials, and Colorado Authors' League. She is a Laureate of both the Colorado Aviation and the Women's Halls of Fame, graduate of Temple University, Columbia College (Distinguished Alumna Award Winner), and the University of Nebraska (Alumni Achievement Award Winner). She is a member of numerous aviation and writers organizations. A General Aviation pilot, she co-holds a World's Aviation Speed Record. With advanced degrees and extensive broadcast experience, she is a frequent speaker for the aviation industry with a passion for aviation history. Learn more at www.PennyHamilton.com

Other books by Penny Rafferty Hamilton, Ph.D.

- *A to Z: Your Grand County History Alphabet* (2017)

- *Absent Aviators: Gender Issues in Aviation* (Chapter contributor 2016)

- *Images of America: Around Granby* (2013)

- *Granby, Then & Now: 1905 - 2005* (2005)